AIRBUS

A340 AND A330

GUY NORRIS AND MARK WAGNER

MBI Publishing Company

First published in 2001 by MBI Publishing Company
Galtier Plaza, Suite 200, 380 Jackson Street,
St. Paul, MN 55101-3885 USA

MBI Publishing Company books are also available at discounts in bulk
quantity for industrial or sales-promotional use. For details write to
Special Sales Manager at Motorbooks International Wholesalers &
Distributors, Galtier Plaza, Suite 200, 380 Jackson Street,
St. Paul, MN 55101-3885 USA

Library of Congress Cataloging-in-Publication Data Available
ISBN 0-7603-0889-6

Edited by Michael Haenggi

Printed in China

About the Authors: Guy Norris is the Los Angeles based west
coast editor of *Flight International* magazine.

Mark Wagner is Chief Photographer of *Flight International* based
out of London, UK.

On the front cover: Pictured moments after touchdown at its
first port of call outside France, the prototype A340 taxis to the
stand at the Singapore airshow in February 1992. The short visit
was intended to be a lot more than a publicity stunt, and
doubled as a serious test of the aircraft's long-range cruise
performance. Given the importance of SIA's order, the visit also
carried tremendous diplomatic weight.

On the frontispiece: With vital sales victories in Europe, the
Middle East, and Asia (particularly Singapore), already under its
belt, Airbus was in jubilant mood when it celebrated the roll-out
of the first A340 at Toulouse on October 4, 1991.

On the title page: Air France introduced its first A340-300s
into revenue service in late March 1992, replacing Boeing 747s
on the Paris-Washington route. It followed with twice-weekly
A340 Paris-Mexico services, along with five-times weekly Paris-
Houston-Mexico flights. By August that year Paris was linked by
A340 with Buenos Aires, Argentina. Services to Santiago, Chile,
and Recife and Sao Paulo, Brazil, followed by the end of 1992.

On the back cover: The full 245 feet 11 inch length of the
A340-600 is readily apparent from this side view captured at the
2001 Paris air show. Compared to the –300, the –600
incorporates a 10-frame fuselage plug forward of the wing and a
single frame extension just over the wing leading edge.

CONTENTS

CHAPTER ONE

FULFILLING THE DREAM

Illuminated by late summer sunlight, the world's longest jetliner slowly emerged from the giant Airbus Industrie assembly building at Toulouse in France. Even to the workers gathered there that afternoon in September 2000, the new aircraft looked staggeringly huge. It seemed a fitting way to mark three decades of hard work and remarkable achievements.

A classic state-of-the-art jetliner in Europe during the 1960s was the Aerospatiale (Sud-Aviation) SE.210 Caravelle. Developed originally by the Sud-Est company, it was the world's first rear engine-mounted jet airliner and the first short-haul aircraft of its type to go into production. Although continuously developed throughout the 1960s to eventually seat up to 140, it was totally inadequate for the coming air traffic boom. This CTA example, pictured still going strong at Zurich, Switzerland, in 1988, was eventually sold to Latin American operators in the 1990s.

The super long airliner was the A340-600, a giant by any standards, measuring more than 245 feet in length. Larger than Boeing's 777-300, the 747-400, and within a foot of Lockheed Martin's leviathan C-5 Galaxy, it represented to some the penultimate expression of an audacious European dream, which sought to challenge the incontestable might of the American aerospace industry.

The A340-600 was considered "penultimate" because only three months later Airbus formally launched the A380, a 550-plus seat giant jetliner to overcome Boeing's dominance of the jumbo market with the 747. The A380, formerly dubbed the A3XX, together with the new breed of A340 models, would form the gauntlet of Airbus Industrie's

Previous Page: A dream fulfilled, as Airbus' dynamic duo, the A330 and A340 crisscross the clear blue desert skies at the Dubai air show in 1993. The development of these large, advanced jetliners marked the maturity of Airbus as a commercial manufacturer, and provided a crucial "big jet" bridgehead to the launch of the A380 jumbo in the twenty-first century.

attack on the high capacity end of the market for the first decade of the twenty-first century.

It all seemed a huge leap for an organization that had been created out of almost nothing just thirty years earlier. The official birthday was December 18, 1970, when Airbus Industrie was formally constituted as a groupement d'interet economique (GIE), under French law. The fledgling organization had established itself at offices in the Avenue de Versailles in Paris with lots of ideas, but little else. The GIE possessed no factory to build any aircraft, had no products, no huge sums of money, and only a handful of staff.

These were led by Roger Beteille, the former head of the flight test department at Sud-Est Aviation and now, in 1970, senior vice president, technical and program coordination at Airbus. His newly appointed chairman was Henri Zeigler, who had moved from the newly created Aerospatiale where he was also chairman. Zeigler, formerly with Sud-Aviation, had taken a leading role in the development of the Anglo-French Concorde supersonic airliner project.

Both knew they faced what to some seemed an almost hopeless task. Airbus was launched in an atmosphere of global

The largest short-haul jetliner developed by the British throughout the pre-Airbus era was the de Havilland, later Hawker-Siddeley Trident. Sadly compromised by being tied exclusively to the design requirements of the national carrier, British European Airways, the Trident was not a best-seller with total sales eventually reaching 115. The ultimate version, pictured here, was the Trident 3 capable of seating 180 passengers. It was through the wing-building expertise of Hawker-Siddeley, however, that Britain maintained a stake in Airbus even after the U.K. government had formally withdrawn from the project.

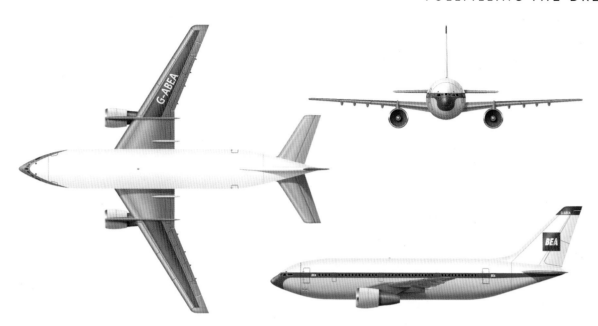

The HBN.100 illustrated here never made it further than the drawing board, but can still be considered as the genetic ancestor of the Airbus A300 and its wide-body successors.

upheaval, dramatic change, and new innovation. Earlier in 1970, U.S. troops had invaded Cambodia, extending the crisis in Asia to new levels, yet that year the world also witnessed the almost unbelievable rescue of the Apollo 13 astronauts. Rock fans had reeled as the Beatles broke up, while followers mourned the premature death of Jimi Hendrix. Italian soccer fans, beaten in the World Cup final by Brazil, consoled themselves with Simon and Garfunkel's "Bridge Over Troubled Water" the record of the year, while moviegoers flocked to see an epic called *Airport*. Technology marched forward as IBM introduced data storage devices called "floppy discs" and in Switzerland the liquid crystal display was being invented.

If ever the founders of Airbus believed there was a time to launch a challenge to the established world order, it seemed this was it. Besides, the key market for its proposed jetliner was right there in Europe. The groundswell leading to the formation of the GIE had started in Britain, France, and Germany over the previous decade. All three countries had seen a huge expansion in the mass market for jet travel, and European airlines quickly saw the need for a larger type of airliner on their short-to-medium route structures. They wanted something with around 200-plus seats that would be a kind of "airbus."

Worried by forecasts of an explosion in traffic by the 1970s, the airlines embarked on a series of informal meetings that began at the Paris air show in June 1965. Air France, Alitalia, British European Airways (BEA), Lufthansa, Sabena, and SAS all met to discuss what they hoped might turn into common requirements.

At the same time, sensing the first signs of an opportunity, French and German aircraft companies also got together at the show to discuss potential joint ventures. French companies, particularly Breguet and Nord-Aviation, the latter soon to be merged with Sud to form Aerospatiale, had studied wide-bodied jetliner concepts and were keen to capitalize on the success of the Caravelle.

The German companies had no sooner returned home when, on July 2, 1965, they announced the formation of an "airbus study group," or Studiengruppe Airbus. This was the first time the phrase "airbus" had appeared. The group included ATG Siebelwerke, Bolkow, Dornier, Flugzeug-union Sud, HFB, Messerschmitt, and VFW. By December of that year, the German group was formalized as the Arbeitsgemeinschaft (Arge) Airbus, creating a unit that would be a partner in any future international venture. In later years this would become known as Deutsche Airbus.

The never-to-be-forgotten sight of an Aero Spacelines-developed Super Guppy at Manchester, United Kingdom, collecting yet another set of Airbus wings. The rather grotesque Super Guppy, named for a species of bloated Caribbean fish, was originally developed for the U.S. space program. However, a small fleet found lasting employment as the air bridge between Airbus partners. Originally derived from the Boeing 377, the use of these unusual aircraft spawned the old joke that every Airbus began its life in the belly of a Boeing!

The airlines meanwhile met again in London that October and failed to reach any consensus. The meeting did, however, lead to the establishment of an Anglo-French Ministry Working Party that was tasked with looking at the prospects for an "air bus." In November 1965 the group published its report called Outline Specification for the High-Capacity Short-Haul Aircraft. The document effectively formed a blueprint for the requirements that would be used to ultimately shape the first airbus, the A300.

The report called for an aircraft seating between 200 and 225, with direct operating costs 30 percent lower than the Boeing 727-100 over a range of 800-plus nautical miles. A subsequent refinement modified this to a 225-seater with a range of 1,200 nautical miles. A crucial aspect of the report was the inclusion of two of the newest generation, high-bypass ratio turbofans as the recommended powerplants. It suggested either the Pratt & Whitney JT9D, then in early development for the 747-100, or the proposed Rolls-Royce RB.178—a twin spool configuration that was ultimately abandoned in favor of the three-shaft RB.207, forerunner of the eventual RB.211.

It was against this proactive, government-influenced background that the British and French aircraft makers began to explore the opportunity for collaboration. Hawker-Siddeley (HS), linked with Breguet and Nord-Aviation to form the HBN group. This studied five baseline configurations dubbed the HBN.100 to 104, the most orthodox of which was the twin-engined, 225- to 260-seat HBN.100. This was sketched around a 20-foot wide fuselage giving it commonality with the 747, technical details of which had only recently been revealed.

Sud-Aviation meanwhile continued studies of larger widebodied aircraft under its Grosse Julie (Fat Julie) project. These were refined into a project called the Galion that was itself later tailored to suit the requirements established by the U.K.-French working group. Unlike the HBN.100, which featured high bypass ratio turbofans mounted prominently on pylons jutting from beneath the leading edge, the Galion looked more like a Dassault Mercure or 737 on steroids.

January 1966 saw a significant turn of events when the first meeting of government officials from Britain, France, and Germany took place. Three national partners were

American Airlines changed the history of air transport in April 1966 when it issued a requirement for a 250- to 300-seat "air bus" aircraft with the same range and field performance as the 727. The requirement led directly to the birth of the DC-10, which American launched in 1968, as well as to the competing Lockheed L-1011 TriStar. It also provided the European study group with the perfect blueprint for an "airbus" of its own, though with a few notable changes including the notion of a wide-body twin.

announced: Hawker-Siddeley, Sud-Aviation and Arge Airbus, while the HBN.100 was picked as the baseline design. The first formal meeting at company board level took place in September, and in October 1966 a formal application for the necessary funding was made to the three governments. The application came with a brochure describing an aircraft called A-300, or Airbus seating 300. The birth of the first Airbus was under way.

Defining An "Airbus"

The pace of developments accelerated through 1967 as the A300 began to grow in size. The fuselage diameter grew to 21 feet, providing space for up to 320 passengers. The size began to outstrip the available power being promised by Pratt & Whitney's JT9D, which it projected would be around

47,500 pounds thrust by 1975. Growth prospects were meanwhile sustained by Rolls-Royce's "paper" RB.207 engine, which the manufacturer expected would be capable of 50,000 pounds thrust and more.

The first "Airbus" meeting at government minister level took place in Paris on May 9, 1967. It was aimed at sanctioning the launch of a "joint project definition study of the best aircraft capable of being built around two such [RB.207] engines." The meeting was attended by U.K. Minister of State for Technology, John Stonehouse, with French Minister of State for Foreign Affairs, Andre Bettencourt, and West German State Secretary at the Economics Ministry, Dr. Johann Schollhorn.

The meeting estimated the overall market potential was around 250 aircraft, but specified that the launch orders had

Proposed "Two-Eleven" and "Three-Eleven" developments of the BAC (British Aircraft Corporation) "One-Eleven" distracted U.K. government interest in the Airbus project. Ultimately these studies never materialized as real aircraft, though U.K. production of BAC 1-11s continued into the late 1970s with more than 220 produced. This wide-body "Three-Eleven" concept features the "10-ton" CFM56 engine which, ironically, would later power the A340.

to come from the three national airlines, Air France, BEA, and Lufthansa. It also divided up airframe research and development costs with Britain (HS) and France (Sud-Aviation) each receiving 37.5 percent of a total sum of 190 million U.K. pounds. Arge Airbus, representing Germany, was to receive the balance of 25 percent.

Estimated costs of 60 million U.K. pounds for the engine were also divided up with Rolls-Royce (R-R) earmarked to receive 75 percent, while 12.5 percent was to go to SNECMA of France, and 12.5 percent to MAN of Germany. In return for the high proportion of engine research and development funding, the British government also agreed to cede leadership of the airframe project to France.

By that summer the definition study was completed and delegates met at Lancaster House, London, on July 25, 1967, for the vital meeting that would pave the way for the Airbus project to begin. This time Stonehouse and Schollhorn were joined by French Transport Minister Jean Chamant to sign a mission statement. This read: "For the purpose of strengthening European cooperation in the field of aviation technology and thereby promoting economic and technological progress in Europe, to take appropriate measures for the joint development and production of an air bus."

The project received its formal go-ahead on September 26, 1967, when an intergovernmental memorandum of understanding (MoU) established that detail design would begin in June 1968. The MoU also established that the "A-300" would not be launched unless the three national airlines agreed together to buy a minimum of 75 aircraft. Of the three nations, it was Britain that pressed most strongly for this stipulation and, unfortunately for the United Kingdom, this would eventually have dramatic repercussions.

The A-300 meanwhile continued to grow with overall length increasing from 160 feet in mid-1967 to almost 177 feet a year later. But airline interest in the aircraft became inversely proportional to its length. The larger it got, the less they were interested. Worse still, one of the largest targets, American Airlines, committed to a trijet design for a classic air bus role for which it had issued the original specification in April 1966.

The U.S. airline wanted an aircraft with the same range and field performance as the 727, but with twice the passenger load. It wanted an air bus that could carry a full load, plus 5,000 pounds of cargo from Chicago to Los Angeles at Mach 0.8. It wanted the aircraft to be able to fly 1,850 nautical miles from a 9,000-foot runway. However, for shorter routes, say

Three key target airlines for the fledgling Airbus project included guaranteed sales to Air France, British European Airways (BEA), and Lufthansa. The latter was the European launch customer for the Boeing 727, one of whose –200s is pictured here. Despite Lufthansa's enthusiasm for Boeing and McDonnell Douglas products (Lufthansa also flew the 707, 720, 737, 747, and DC-10), it later committed to every member of the Airbus family with the exception of the A330.

from New York to Chicago, the same aircraft would have to operate in high temperatures with a full load from short runways such as those at La Guardia Airport, New York.

The specification, devised by the airline's influential president Frank Kolk, appeared to be tailor-made to the big, twin-engined air bus design being considered in Europe. The U.S. manufacturers were not prepared to let vague paper projects from Europe get in their way, however, and both Douglas and Lockheed came up with a host of new designs for "Kolk machines" as they were nicknamed.

Although the first of these were predominantly twins, concerns over reliability, engine-out ferry capability, and climb out performance from cities like Denver soon turned both aircraft makers to trijets. The outcome was the birth of both the McDonnell Douglas DC-10 and Lockheed L-1011 TriStar, the former of which was launched with an American Airlines order in February 1968. Ironically, it was only Airbus that stuck to the original American specification for a large twin. This decision eventually paved the way for success for Airbus, and later Boeing, which wholeheartedly adopted the big twin concept. The universal popularity of big twins ultimately contributed to the downfall of both Lockheed and McDonnell Douglas as manufacturers of commercial jetliners.

The birth of the TriStar also diverted the attention of R-R away from the RB.207 and the A-300. Instead it focused on the development of the RB.211 for the U.S. trijet, and forced the original Airbus team to consider more realistically available engines already in production or development. These engines were mainly the General Electric CF6-50, in development for the DC-10, and the JT9D-15.

To make matters worse, BEA, the British airline expected to help launch the A-300, was becoming more interested in a proposed competitor called the Two-Eleven and a follow-on derivative, the even larger Three-Eleven. The concept was a family of T-tail, twin-engined wide-bodies derived from the original British Aircraft Corporation (BAC) One-Eleven. Powered by RB.211 engines, BEA believed the Two-Eleven offered a thoroughly homegrown answer to its needs without having to adopt a more compromised design adapted to the needs of two other airlines.

June 1968 came and went without a single order. Getting more anxious, the Airbus team under Beteille increasingly looked to designs using the alternative, proven U.S. engines rather than the R-R option. The result was a slightly smaller design seating about 250. The revised design was dubbed the "A-300B" instead of the A-250, and had a smaller fuselage

One of the earliest-built Airbus products still in service in the 1990s was this Air France A300B2-1A/1C variant. First flown on June 23, 1974, aircraft number 006 was delivered to the airline three days later and plied the European skies continuously for the remaining 23 years of its operational life.

diameter as well as shorter length. Diameter was reduced to 18 feet 6 inches and overall length to 158 feet 6 inches. Maximum takeoff weight was also slashed back to 275,000 pounds, a reduction of about 50,000 pounds.

The redesign revived optimism about the aircraft's long term viability amongst French and German industry partners, but further alienated British interests that were strongly tied to those of R-R. As 1969 wound on, it soon became obvious that the British government was losing interest in the project. BEA was showing little enthusiasm for the aircraft its own government had originally instructed it to order and, on top of this, the anti-European sentiments of the Technology Minister, Anthony Wedgwood Benn, did little to help. Amidst scenes of some acrimony, the United Kingdom made the shock announcement on April 10 that it was withdrawing.

The shock was particularly devastating for Hawker-Siddeley which, by this time, had virtually completed the design of the A-300 wing and was tooled up to begin production. The British company was out on a limb without the support of its own government, but so was Airbus. Neither Sud-Aviation nor Deutsche Airbus had the resources to fund the development and design of an entirely new wing. Both French and German partners also conceded that the best expertise for such work existed in the United Kingdom.

Worst of all, it could not afford the delay of more than a year that was expected to be entailed in finding an alternative.

Rescue came in the form of a deal orchestrated by German Defense Minister, Franz-Josef Strauss. Using his influence with the Finance Ministry, Strauss devised an arrangement under which West Germany funded 60 percent of the development costs of the wing. This indirect subsidy, accounting for around DM250 million (more than $150 million), was provided to Hawker-Siddeley in exchange for a fixed price contract to supply main structural wing boxes for the prototypes, an option for future wing sets, and continuing responsibility for wing design and development.

Funding for the balance of the deal, signed in July 1969, was raised by Hawker-Siddeley itself. The company's courageous move helped the United Kingdom retain a foothold in Airbus, albeit a privately owned one, and kept open a vital door through which it would later rejoin the enterprise as a full national player. In the meantime, however, Airbus was restructured to reflect the departure of the United Kingdom and the entry of new partners.

Launching Airbus

Within a month of the British withdrawal, French Minister Chamant and German Minister Schiller signed agreements to proceed with the development of the A-300, each nation assuming 50 percent of the project. As the first parts of the aircraft, now called the A300B, began to come together, so did the first of the new partners. The Netherlands government took a 6.6 percent share of the aircraft through Fokker-VFW in December 1970. The German and French share of production was 36.5 percent while the United Kingdom's share, through Hawker-Siddeley, was 20 percent.

Despite the involvement of the United Kingdom and the Netherlands in the production of the aircraft itself, France and Germany retained 50 percent each of the overall shares in the consortium. This changed in October 1971 when CASA of Spain joined Airbus taking a 4.2 percent stake, reducing the holdings of the two existing partners to 47.9 percent each. Eight years later, these shares were again reduced to 37.9 percent when the United Kingdom rejoined the consortium as a full member through British Aerospace (BAe). Hawker-Siddeley, until then the sole U.K. member, had become merged with BAC in 1977 to form BAe and the combined group assumed a 20 percent share in Airbus on January 1, 1979.

With the complication of Rolls-Royce's "paper" engine removed from the scene, Airbus formally selected GE's CF6-50A as lead engine on the A300B. This created some commonality with the DC-10 that made its maiden flight on August 29, 1970. Zeigler knew Airbus needed to save as much time and money as it could, particularly with the redesign of the A300B, and in a bold move approached McDonnell Douglas over the possibilities of collaboration.

Far from being wary, the U.S. company appeared keen to help and even offered to sell Airbus ready-made fuselage barrels. However, a deal was struck over the engine nacelle and pylon design, areas that would have been enormously expensive and time-consuming for Airbus to have tackled from scratch. General Electric also agreed to cut a deal with the Airbus partner countries, allowing almost 40 percent of the value of each engine to be made in France and Germany.

SNECMA took 22 percent of parts manufacture, plus a further 6 percent for the value of assembly work at its Corbeil site, and testing at Villaroche. MTU in Germany was given responsibility for the high pressure (HP) turbine, valued at 11

Swissair help launch the second Airbus model, the A310-200, into production when it and Lufthansa placed orders in July 1978. The A310 incorporated a more advanced wing profile that would later form the blueprint for the aerodynamics of the A330/A340 wing. It also ushered in advanced "glass" cockpit displays, composite materials in secondary structure, and electrical signaling of some secondary controls. Development of the later A310-300 saw further use of composites in primary structures, particularly the tail fin, carbon brakes, and the use of a tail trim fuel tank for center-of-gravity control.

Another wave of advanced technology swept into operational service with the introduction of the A320 in 1988. The major breakthroughs included a fly-by-wire flight control system, side-stick controller in the cockpit, active flight controls, and a second-generation digital autoflight system. All these features, added to extensive use of composites and advanced aluminum alloys, would be baselined in the new A330 and A340.

percent of the whole. This was later adjusted to give SNECMA 27 percent, MTU 12 percent, and GE 61 percent.

Construction of the prototype was by now well under way at Aerospatiale's Toulouse-Blagnac airport facility, where it was decided all Airbus final assembly should be concentrated. A unique production system was also devised to feed the line with large subassemblies from the main partners as well as suppliers all over the world.

The backbone of the system was the Aero Spacelines-developed Super Guppy 201—a bizarrely enlarged derivative of the Boeing 377, designed originally to carry sections of Saturn space rockets for the Apollo moon project. The balloon-like Super Guppy could swallow up whole wings and entire chunks of fuselage in its cavernous interior that measured 25 feet 6 inches wide.

A single Super Guppy began the first shuttle of parts between the Airbus partner sites in 1972. It ferried completed

wings from Chester in the United Kingdom, via Manchester International Airport, to MBB's Bremen facility in Germany. Fuselage assemblies were flown down from Hamburg to Toulouse, while other sections were flown to Aerospatiale's Saint-Nazaire site in Nantes for completion. The Super Guppy, which was soon joined by a second, also plodded sedately south to Madrid where it collected the horizontal tail section, elevators, and doors from CASA before heading back north over the Pyrenees to Toulouse.

Meanwhile, in September 1970, Air France became the first airline to signal firm interest in the A300. It wanted the aircraft for its high-density shuttle-type services between Paris, London, Geneva, and Corsica, and signed a letter of intent for six. It also agreed to hold a further 10 on option, and firmed up the whole deal in November 1971.

Almost immediately Air France became a strong influence on the first design evolution of the A300B. The airline considered the initial 250-seat A300B1 version too small, even though it had yet to fly, and more powerful engines were in the works that would allow room for growth. At the request of Air France, Airbus therefore began studies of a slightly stretched version that was extended by five fuselage frames, making it 8 feet 7 inches longer than the A300B1. The longer body of the A300B2, as it was called, allowed for an additional three seat rows, or 24 seats, and this would form the basic standard for the first production aircraft. A longer-range derivative of the B2, called the B4, was also proposed.

The B2 version was 177 feet 5 inches long, weighed 302,000 pounds, and was designed to carry 281 passengers versus the 257 mixed-class seating capacity of the original B1. The B4, with provision for a center fuel tank in the wing box, was configured with a maximum takeoff weight of 330,700 pounds. This version was ultimately delivered as the B4-100, with a higher weight (363,760-pound) B4-200 following soon after.

Other versions planned included an intermediate weight A300B3, a B5 freighter, a B6 stretch freighter, a B7 with a slight stretch of the B2 powered by the RB.211-61 engine, and a lighter weight B8 aimed at the U.S. market. The long-range road map also outlined a vague reference to a longer range B9, which as will be seen, would ultimately evolve as the A330. The B3, B5, B6, B7, and B8 were, however, never to fly.

Construction of the B1 meanwhile continued and this was rolled out on September 28, 1972—almost five years to the day after the program had received its official go-ahead in 1967. A month later, on October 28, a team of five including Max Fischl, Bernard Ziegler, Romeo Zinzoni, Pierre Caneill, and Gunther Scherer, flew the A300 for the first time. Departing Toulouse in sunshine, the aircraft was airborne for 1 hour 25 minutes, during which a maximum speed of 185 knots was reached at an altitude of 14,000 feet. The flight, which included cycling of the flaps and undercarriage, was judged a great success and boded well for the program.

The second airframe off the line was doomed never to fly, and instead rolled away to become the static test article at the Centre d'Essais Aeronautiques de Toulouse (CEAT). The third airframe, registered F-WUAC, became the second, and last A300B1, joining the flight test program on February 5, 1973. The fourth airframe was sent to MBB in Germany for fatigue testing.

The fifth and sixth airframes were the first two B2s, and therefore the first production standard aircraft. Registered F-

WUAD and UAA respectively, they flew on June 28 and November 20, 1973. Two months later, in January 1974, Airbus opened its Toulouse-Blagnac offices as the test program accelerated. By early spring the four flight test aircraft had amassed 1,580 hours in a virtually trouble-free program. The French DGAC and German LBA certification authorities awarded Airbus with type certification for the A300B2 on March 15, 1974, and the U.S. Federal Aviation Administration (FAA) followed suit on May 30.

The first production aircraft A300B2, officially A300 number 5, made its maiden flight on April 15, 1974, and was handed over to Air France on May 10. After almost two weeks of training, Air France inaugurated commercial airline service with the A300 on May 23, 1974, when it carried 25 first- and 225 economy-class passengers from Paris to London. The age of the Airbus had finally begun.

Family Planning

By the end of 1974 a total of five A300s had entered service with three airlines, including the second B1 on lease to Trans European Airlines (TEA). The first A300B4, A300 number 9, flew on December 26, 1974, and was certificated on March 26, 1975. The first B4 was delivered to Frankfurt-based charter company, Germanair, later merged into Hapag Lloyd, on May 23.

Despite the promising start, Airbus faced a bleak-looking future. The aircraft was a technical success, but a marketing headache, particularly in the key U.S. market where it was regarded almost as a joke. To add to these problems, the global economy was in the midst of recession following the 1973 oil crisis, and airliner sales were slow the world over. Between 1974 and 1976, the A300 order book increased by only 18. However, during the next three years sales increased by 152 as the health of the world economy began to improve.

By this stage Pratt & Whitney's JT9D engine became a firm option on the A300, launched by SAS in February 1978. The first P&W-powered Airbus flew in April 1979, and was delivered to SAS the following January. Meanwhile, the RB.211 was also theoretically available on the A300, though it was never selected.

All this time, Airbus maintained vigilant studies for its all-important family plan. It knew right from the start that the key to long-term survival, and success, was the establishment of a broad-based family of products with which to satisfy the airlines. Although handicapped from the start with only two basic derivatives of its single A300 product, Airbus focused increasing energy on the next most likely family member.

At first this was expected to be a larger capacity, short- to medium-range twin, but the same fuel crisis that paralyzed the A300B order book also killed off these plans. Instead, focus shifted to a shortened A300 with reduced passenger capacity called the A300B10. By June 1975, this proposal was gathering pace and was outlined as a 14-frame shrink of the baseline A300, seating around 214.

Throughout 1976, the design began to drift away from the A300 and assumed distinctive characteristics of its own. A new, smaller purpose-built wing was designed and changes were incorporated into the fuselage. The final product was the A310, launched in July 1978 on the back of commitments from Air France, Swissair, and Lufthansa, for 35 aircraft. Initially Airbus planned two versions, the regional A310-100 and an intercontinental –200. The former had a range of 2,000 nautical miles with 210 passengers, while the latter had a center section fuel tank, a higher gross weight, and could carry the same load an additional 1,000 nautical miles.

Swissair was the first to place firm orders in March 1979, and was soon followed by Lufthansa, KLM, Martinair Holland, Sabena, Air France, and Air Afrique. By the time the development aircraft made its first flight on April 3, 1982, orders and options had been placed for 181 aircraft by 15 airlines. These were all for the –200 version, and Airbus decided to stop offering the –100, none of which were built. The aircraft received European certification in March 1983 and entered service with Lufthansa and Swissair on April 12 and April 21, respectively.

Airlines continued to demand more range, and in response Airbus devised tail fuel tanks for a new version dubbed the –300. Higher thrust GE and P&W engines were made available for the long-range variant that soon became more popular than the –200. The first –300 was delivered to Swissair on December 16, 1985, and by the late 1990s the –300 was considered the standard production version.

With the A310 well under way, Airbus turned its attention next to the single-aisle market. Boeing and McDonnell Douglas dominated this arena with the 737/757 and the -DC-9/MD-80 families respectively, but Airbus realized that it was vital to offer airlines a family of its own. In 1980 it established a single-aisle (SA) study team at Toulouse, headed by Derek Brown, a former team leader of the Joint European Transport (JET)—an international project aimed at a family

of aircraft between 130 and 188 passengers. The SA studies were divided into three aircraft ranging from 125 to 180 seats, dubbed the SA1, SA2, and SA3.

In February 1981, the SA projects were re-designated under the name "A320" with an initial focus on the 150-seat SA2. The SA1 would later emerge as the A319, while the SA3 was to become the A321. Working closely with Delta Air Lines and the U.S. carrier's "Delta III" requirement for a new 150-seater, Airbus tailored the A320 to suit the American market. The new link immediately led to a renewed design focus on the larger of two proposed A320 variants.

Although Delta never ordered the A320, opting for the MD-90 instead, the relationship had enormous benefits for the credibility of the design that was slightly wider than the competing Boeing narrow bodies as a result. Coming into a highly competitive market, Airbus realized it needed extra benefits; additional cabin width was essential. Others included a whole range of advanced technology features such as a fly-by-wire (FBW) flight control system, as well as other structural and systematic innovations.

The decision to plump for the A320 as the next project, rather than a long-range quad-jet being pushed by German industry, almost caused a major rift between the Airbus partners. However, the rapid growth of the A320 order book and subsequent expansion of the family, later led to the establishment of a second Airbus production line in Hamburg, somewhat appeasing earlier German resentment. This assembled A319s and A321s and, by January 2001, the German line had produced its 500th Airbus.

Air France again became the first airline to sign its name against a new Airbus product and, at the 1981 Paris air show, announced a letter of intent for 25 aircraft. Others soon followed including Air Inter, British Caledonian, Cyprus Airways, and Inex Adria. Of these, British Caledonian became the first to place a firm order when it signed for seven in October 1983.

Throughout this period, Airbus struggled to secure the $200 million in development funding it needed to launch the A320. It was not until March 1984 that this was in place and approval was granted by the Airbus Board to begin full-scale development. The following October the aircraft, and Airbus as a whole, got probably the biggest boost in its history when Northwest Airlines signed an order for up to 100 A320s.

The A320 was rolled out at a spectacular celebration in Toulouse on February 14, 1987, and flew for the first time

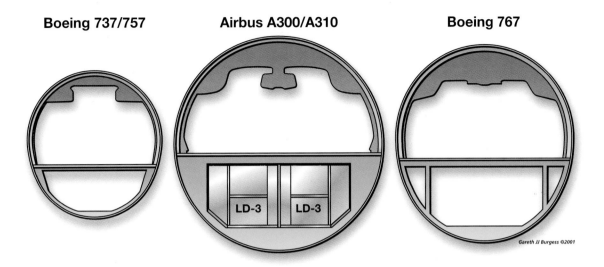

Boeing 737/757   **Airbus A300/A310**   **Boeing 767**

LD-3   LD-3

Gareth JJ Burgess ©2001

Early performance requirement studies for a European "air bus" were set against the template of the Boeing 727-100. Targets included dramatic reductions in direct operating costs per seat, and a virtual doubling of passenger and cargo capacity.

eight days later. At the time of the rollout, the A320 had orders and commitments for 439 aircraft, against just 15 for the original A300 back in 1972. Test flying progressed smoothly, despite the high-tech FBW and other systems, and certification was awarded on February 26, 1988. In all, the four aircraft in the test effort accumulated more than 1,200 hours on 530 flights.

Airbus had another reason to celebrate as the A320 was unveiled. Just a few days earlier, in January 1987, Lufthansa had become the first airline to commit to the next member of the growing Airbus family. It signed a deal covering the purchase of up to 30 of the new, long-range four-engined aircraft Airbus called the A340. Two months later the twin-engined A330 was launched with orders from Air Inter and Thai Airways International. Airbus, it seemed, was at last on the verge of completing its family, and the full-scale development of the most ambitious jetliner twin program in the history of the industry was about to begin.

First of the many. The prototype A300B pictured on its maiden flight on October 28, 1972 over the French countryside near Toulouse. The most significant teething problems unearthed during these early flights were concerned with the autopilot and the flaps, the latter tending to jam on retraction due to friction. The test effort was, nonetheless, a textbook operation which was two months ahead of schedule by the following February.

CHAPTER TWO

BIRTH OF A NEW FAMILY

t was a news editor's dream. Airbus finally announced the long-awaited go-ahead of the A330 and A340 programs on a hot, thundery day in June 1987, the week before the start of the Paris air show.

Airbus got two distinct answers when it began asking airlines whether the new large jetliner should have two engines or four. North American carriers predominantly favored twins, while virtually all the Asian airlines wanted quads. Although somewhat blurred in recent years, this geographic split is still evident two decades on and is illustrated here by a Canadian-based Skyservice-operated A330-300 (on previous page), and a China Southwest A340.

The stories at the show revolved not only around the launch itself, and the effect of the big new jets on the industry, but also on the fact that they had been launched as one program. This highly unusual step held major significance for the cost, design, and marketability of both aircraft. The decision to launch them together meant a savings of half a billion U.S. dollars over the cost of launching them separately.

Speaking about the choice in 1991, the charismatic Airbus managing director at the time, Jean Pierson, recalled,

". . . there was a debate within Airbus. Some people said we should launch a twin, others a quad. Finally the engineers promised they could do both with a common airframe for half a billion less. So I said, 'Let's go!'"

The move made a lot of sense financially, even if it caused some concern that aspects of the designs may have to be compromised. It was a lot easier, he said, to sell a $3.5 billion combined program to the governments than it would have been to return to them in two years and ask for another $1.5 billion to launch a second aircraft.

More than any previous Airbus project, the A330/340 was designed to maximize market share and revenue. "The A330 and A340 do not represent a technology goal," said Pierson, quoted in Flight International magazine in May 1991. "The goal is to increase market share, and using the technology of the A320, to make money with that share. It is a business goal. When you launch an aircraft you have to decide your priorities. These aircraft have already helped us to increase our market share from 20 percent to 30 percent in the last four years. We've sold more than 200 aircraft of both types, and the A340 is not due to fly for five months."

Pierson personally steered the A330 and A340 toward launch from 1985 when he was appointed managing director. As Pierson had witnessed first-hand the intense internal debates over whether to go with the big twin or the quad, one of his first tasks was the establishment of a team to focus on the issues. The team soon discovered that it was not only Airbus that was divided on the issue—so was the airline world.

Adam Brown, vice president for strategic planning during the crucial years of the A330/A340 and later A3XX/A380 programs recalled, ". . . North American operators were clearly in

Another ingredient behind the birth of the A340 was the promise of a new generation of "10-ton" turbofans like the CFM56. However, after years of test and development, the GE-SNECMA joint venture engine failed to attract a single commercial order and by 1979 its future was in doubt. Luckily for Airbus, the CFM56 survived by a hair when it was selected by United Airlines over a competing Pratt & Whitney alternative to power reengined DC-8s. The order came within two weeks of the engine's cancellation, and eventually covered the reengining of 110 DC-8s, one of which is pictured in later life as a freighter with TAMPA Colombia.

favor of a twin, while the Asians wanted a quad. In Europe, opinion was split between the two. The majority of potential customers were in favor of a quad despite the fact, in certain conditions, it is more costly to operate than a twin. They liked that it could be ferried with one engine out, and could fly 'anywhere'—remember ETOPS hadn't begun then."

At the time, Airbus was hawking around designs that had evolved from the earliest days of the consortium's existence. The A340's origins could be traced back to the proposed four-engined A300B11 (see chapter 1), a derivative of the short-fuselage B10, which itself was later launched as the A310. The A300B11 built upon the newly available "ten ton" engines then in development in the 1970s, particularly the Franco-U.S. CFM56. Seating about 200 passengers, it was conceived not as the wide-body trijet successor it would become, but as a new-generation replacement for the large world fleets of Boeing 707s and Douglas DC-8s then in service.

The A330's roots went back to the B9, a stretched A300 with the original wing and the most powerful engines then available. The B9 was aimed at the growing demand for high capacity jetliners on medium-range, trans-continental-type trunk routes, and was not projected at long-haul services. Offering the same payload/range as the DC-10, while using up to 25 percent less fuel, the B9 was considered highly attractive.

At the heart of the Airbus concept were studies indicating that, while twins have an operating advantage at lower ranges, the four-engined solution offered better costs on longer missions. The cross-over range at which this transition occurred was about 5,600 nautical miles.

In 1977 came the first of a series of crucial breakthroughs that would lead to the launch of both aircraft as a single program. A design team led by Airbus chief engineer Jean Roder began investigating concepts that would enable both the twin and quad to use the same wing. "Roder was able to create a common wing structure, with the quad's outboard engines providing bending relief to counteract the increased weights of the long-range model. The cost savings this presented enabled us to do both aircraft," says Brown who described the design as "a piece of brilliant insight."

The common wing concept gained ground in 1980 when Airbus restructured its product development strategy to reflect its entry into the narrow body, or single-aisle arena. With the launch of the SA studies (see chapter 1), the original B9 and B11 projects assumed new names. The B9 became the (twin-aisle) TA9, while the B11 became the TA11.

The TA9 was now firmly aimed at the high capacity, short-range markets and was effectively an A300B successor, while the four-engined TA11 was still focused on longer-range missions up to 6,800 nautical miles. The development of the Boeing 757 had meanwhile ushered new engines onto the scene that prompted a set of new studies by Airbus. Several

Key to the success of the A330/A340 program was the common wing. Developed by BAe, the same basic wing was designed to carry either one engine (top) on the A330, or two (bottom) on the A340. The concept dates to 1977 and was the brain child of a design team led by Airbus chief engineer Jean Roder.

Airbus studied larger engines as it explored various twin-aisle (TA11) options. After rejecting wide-body trijet concepts based on Pratt & Whitney JT10D-232s or the similarly sized Rolls-Royce RB.211-535, Airbus later looked at quad jet concepts using the same R-R and P&W powerplants. Interestingly, the resulting A340, if built would have been remarkably similar to the A340-500 that would appear almost 20 years later. By 1986, the TA11 was described by Airbus as a "medium-sized long range four-engined wide-body aircraft featuring a new wing and developments of the A320 propulsion package."

TA11 studies were made using three Rolls-Royce RB.211-535 or Pratt & Whitney JT10D-232 (eventually superseded by the PW2000) engines, to compare them against the four-engined CFM56-powered option. Airbus also outlined a twin-engined derivative of the TA11, the TA12, which would have had around 2,000 nautical miles less range. The TA9, TA11, and TA12 formed what Airbus judged to be a formidable package to compete in the DC-10 and L-1011 replacement market.

By 1982 the finer details of the TA9 design revealed the enormous under-floor cargo potential of the stretched twin that, at this stage, was 27 feet 9 inches longer than the A300. Seating up to 410 in an all-economy layout, the big twin could accommodate 16 LD3s or five pallets in the forward hold and

14 LD3s or four pallets in the aft, or roughly double the capacity of the DC-10/L-1011. Airbus also sketched out a two-member TA9 family, earmarking the TA9-100 designation for short-range 1,500-nautical-mile missions, and the TA9-200 for longer-range routes up to 3,300 nautical miles. The shorter-bodied TA11 was meanwhile illustrated with a range of up to 6,830 nautical miles.

The following year marked the real start of the common program approach when Airbus announced all three projects, including the TA12, would have "largely in common a new wing, center fuselage, main landing gear, and tailplane." The TA11 and TA12 would both use the A310 front and rear fuselage sections, and the TA9 those of the A300-600 in addition

The TA9, as defined in the mid-1980s, was by now taking on the look of the A330, but still retained major elements of the A300-600. Airbus was still focused on developing the large twin for short to medium ranges and could not have foreseen that the shortened, long-range A330-200 would ultimately become the best-selling variant.

to two new "barrels." The aircraft would also use the A300-600 fin and rudder as well as a modified version of the same nose gear.

The TA11 was now envisioned with four 34,000-pound thrust PW2000 or RB.211-535 engines, and was being studied with two fuselage lengths. The shorter TA11-100 had seats for about 230 in tri-class configuration, while the longer TA11-200 seated up to 270 in the same layout.

With the appointment of Pierson in 1985, detailed planning began to accelerate. One of the most dramatic new developments was the proposed use of a "variable camber" wing. Camber is the term describing the cross-sectional curvature of the wing, and is a crucial element of the aerodynamic design. The concept of variable camber, or mission adaptive wings

(MAW), had been examined for several years as a way of improving the efficiency of the aircraft throughout the full speed range.

Wings are generally designed to be at their most efficient in whatever condition the aircraft is expected to spend the most time. A training aircraft is therefore designed with a high-lift wing that performs well at low speeds. A high-flying jetliner is designed with a transonic wing for high-speed cruise. The wing is also fitted with flaps and spoilers that deploy for takeoff and for slow-speed flight during approach and climb out. The idea of the variable camber wing was that the aerodynamic properties of the wing itself could be changed during flight, almost as a bird does by flexing its feathers for landing or gliding.

At the same time in the United States, experiments in next-generation wings were also focused on the MAW principle under a program called the Advanced Fighter Technology Integration (AFTI) effort. The first AFTI experiment was the MAW that was tested on a modified General Dynamics F-111 Transonic Aircraft Technology (TACT) test bed. This had flown as a supercritical NASA test bed in the 1970s and in the mid-1980s was modified again to act as a MAW research vehicle. Internal controls in the MAW physically flexed the wing to adjust the amount of camber to suit the flight conditions. It could flex enough to generate extra lift at slow speeds, eliminating the need for slats and flaps. It could also change into a supercritical wing platform at the flip of a switch for transonic flight, as well as adjust to a near-symmetrical section for supersonic flight.

Airbus aimed for a less dramatic form of variable camber performance, depending on careful control of the existing flaps to change wing shape, rather than altering the wing profile from within. The Airbus concept, originating with work conducted mostly by BAe at Bristol and Hatfield, aimed to produce the effect by pivoting the flaps at their base, rather like moving a double-jointed finger. The flaps would serve their normal function at takeoff and landing, but would have an additional role during cruise when they would be moved out slowly to produce the optimum drag-reducing profile. The change would occur slowly, reflecting the changing altitudes, speeds, and center of gravity shifts of the aircraft as it burned off fuel.

Airbus estimated the feature could generate up to 2 percent gain in aerodynamic efficiency, together with around 1 percent improvement in the high-speed flight margin before the onset of a condition known as Mach buffet. This is caused by the proximity of the speeding aircraft to the sound barrier and the instability that exists in that flight regime. The U.S. MAW tests, which ran from 1985 to 1988, meanwhile, indicated that drag reductions ranged from 8 to 20 percent, depending on particular flight conditions.

Airbus also looked at hybrid laminar flow control to further reduce drag. All aircraft are surrounded by a boundary layer of turbulent air that creates drag and increases fuel consumption. Although wings are very smooth and streamlined, they can never be clean enough to create perfect laminar airflow over the surface. Airbus therefore investigated a system that would provide the wing's upper surface with narrow suction slits aft of the point of maximum thickness. Two slits, cut from tip to tip along the wing, were to provide a flow path for

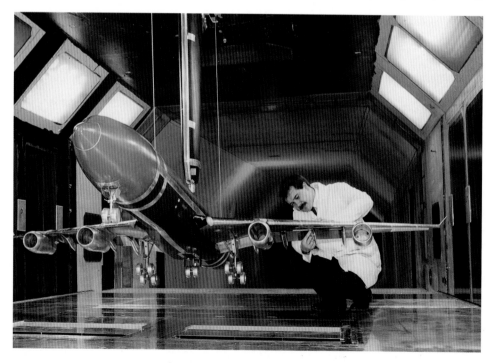

A variable camber wing concept was studied for the new long-range aircraft. The idea was to effectively double-hinge the trailing edge flaps, seen here extended on this wind tunnel model of an A340-300, to enable them to be moved during the cruise. Flight management computers were to have carefully repositioned them to provide the optimum lift-drag profile for differing cruise conditions. Despite expectations of a 2 percent improvement in aerodynamic efficiency, it was later dropped because the cost outweighed the benefits.

By March 1987, Airbus confidently predicted the availability of the IAE V2500 SuperFan on its A340, as pictured in this artist's impression of the aircraft in formation with the A330. The ultra-high bypass geared fan was offered only on the 7,850 nautical miles range A340-300, while the lower capacity –200 version was to be offered with a choice of the SuperFan or CFM56-5 engines. Service entry was expected to be mid-1992.

air to pass from the high-pressure region downstream of the supersonic shockwave to the lower pressure region ahead of it. This would weaken the shockwave, reducing the separation of the turbulent flow, and greatly improving efficiency.

By the time of the Paris show in June 1985, the design of the TA9 and TA11 was being further refined with the adoption of the A320 flight deck, side-stick controls, and a FBW flight control system. At the same time, the TA12 quietly disappeared, never to reappear. The seat-mile cost targets for the quad were also realigned towards the Boeing range. Airbus began promising the seat-mile economy of the 747-300, but with an aircraft that was 50 percent smaller. The TA11 was still aimed at a tri-class payload of around 250 with a maximum range capability of 6,500 nautical miles. Studies of the TA9-100 meanwhile appeared to have been dropped, and all of the focus was on the -200 with a range of 3,200 nautical miles and seats for 330 passengers.

Throughout the next six months it became clear that it was the time to move. On January 27, 1986, the Airbus Industrie Supervisory Board met in Munich and, immediately afterwards,

the board's chairman, Dr. Franz-Josef Strauss, issued a statement. It read: "Airbus Industrie is now in a position to finalize the detailed technical definition of the TA9, which is now officially designated the A330, and the TA11, now called the A340, with potential launch customer airlines, and to discuss with them the terms and conditions for launch commitments."

In reality, the designations were originally reversed. Customer interest was obviously more focused on the TA11, which would have been launched first and was therefore going to be named the A330. The twin was due to follow, so chronologically should have been the A340. However, as Brown recalled, "Our salesmen came back and said that airlines would never get their brains around a twin having a 'four' in its name and the quad not, so we reversed the designations."

Now Airbus began its big push to sign up firm orders for its new offerings. It hoped to attract orders for both the A330 and A340 from around five customers, and on May 12 issued a new set of firm proposals to the most likely candidates. These included Lufthansa and Swissair, both of which were firmly in the market for new-generation long-haul jetliners.

CFM International's long-threatened place on the A340 was secured when it immediately rushed in with the CFM56-5 to fulfill the performance gulf left by the abandonment of the SuperFan project. The change required more adaptations of the low-pressure system but the relatively large capacity of the core (derived from the Rockwell B-1B bomber's GE F101 engine) meant that few modifications were needed to the high-pressure system.

Within weeks of these proposals going out, rumors began circulating of an extraordinary new engine development. International Aero Engines (IAE), which had a memorandum of understanding with Airbus on fitting the V2500-A3 turbofan to the A340, had come up with a revolutionary new engine. Known as the V2500 SuperFan, it was a geared ducted-fan development of the V2500, but would offer fuel savings of up to 15 percent compared to the baseline engine. Crucially, it would also offer up to 32,000 pounds of thrust against the V2500's 28,000 pounds (see chapter 3). The development not only out-classed the competing bid from CFM International (CFMI) with its CFM56-5X, but more significantly from the Airbus perspective, put the A340 well ahead of its closest rival, the three-engined MD-11.

This was a stretched and completely revised version of the popular DC-10, and was aimed at exactly the same market as the A340. According to McDonnell Douglas specifications, the big trijet would carry a typical tri-class load of 276 passengers across ranges of up to 6,900 nautical miles. Range with maximum payload, including a belly full of up to 32 LD3 cargo containers, was expected to be 4,800 nautical miles.

Ironically the SuperFan also put what most considered would be the final nail in the coffin of the proposed collaborative studies between Airbus and McDonnell Douglas that had begun in 1986. These had been prompted by cost concerns in the United Kingdom, particularly after huge losses were incurred during an abortive attempt to develop a new Airborne Early Warning (AEW) system based on the BAe Nimrod. The British company estimated development costs of £840 million for the A330/A340 wing, and could not raise this independently. McDonnell Douglas also encouraged the tie-up, particularly as it secretly feared a gloomy future for its civil jetliner family despite putting a brave face on the MD-11.

McDonnell Douglas Corporation (MDC) chairman, John McDonnell, even visited the government ministers responsible for Airbus in each of the partner companies. He pressed for a collaborative effort aimed squarely at going after Boeing, or as he said, "that big bear in Seattle." A meeting of ministers held in Paris in March 1987 issued a mandate to Airbus to negotiate with MDC on a collaborative product. The nearest these talks got to a firm proposal was a hybrid aircraft dubbed the AM 300 combining the wing of the A330 with the fuselage of the MD-11. The talks later collapsed however, largely due to MDC's dogged determination to stick to its traditional trijet philosophy and an unwillingness by Airbus to subordinate to the Americans. Ironically, had the twin-engined AM 300 proposed by Airbus come to fruition, it would have born a remarkable similarity to the 777 which, at the time, was little more than a twinkle in the eye of Boeing.

In the meantime, more immediate changes were being worked on the A330 design that Airbus announced in late 1986, it would be stretched by five fuselage frames, or 10 feet 7 inches. This allowed another 24 passengers to be seated, but reduced range slightly as a result. At the same time, it was also announced the A340 would have a center section auxiliary undercarriage as standard to allow operations from low-bearing strength runways and taxiways. The center undercarriage leg design had been pioneered by MDC on the DC-10-30.

The SuperFan plan meanwhile gathered speed, and by the time Airbus was given a formal briefing on the engine in late December 1986, it seemed almost certain it would be adopted. International Aero Engines also briefed Boeing on the engine, proposing its use for a 150-seat 7J7 project. The new engine appeared to completely overwhelm CFM that, as recently as October 1986, had signed a memorandum of understanding with Airbus to offer the 28,600-pound thrust CFM56-5 as the primary engine for the A340.

The emergence of the SuperFan had a profound effect on the A340 design that changed virtually overnight to take advantage of the new engine. Airbus hastily redrew the specifications and came up with two versions of the A340, a –200 and a –300. The new engine allowed it to solve the difficult conundrum of how to satisfy two main groups of airlines, one which wanted the same capacity as the original A340 but with more range, and the other that wanted a slightly larger aircraft and not necessarily more range. Airbus claimed the chief difference with both new versions was a distinct operating advantage over the MD-11.

Both versions shared the same design weight, but the A340-300 was 14 feet longer than the A340-200, which retained the same dimensions of the original design. The –200 was sized to carry 262 passengers over a range of 7,850 nauti-cal miles, while the –300 could carry 295 passengers over 7,000 nautical miles.

Even though the claimed fuel burn advantage of the SuperFan gradually reduced to around 10 percent over the baseline V2500-A4, the A340's overall competitiveness was radically improved. For a typical 4,000 nautical miles sector, for example, Airbus claims the A340-300 had a fuel burn per seat advantage of 30 percent over the MD-11! Even more remarkably, this increased to a 42 percent advantage over the proposed MD-11ER version, a 38 percent gain over the 747-300, and a valuable 4 percent over the 747-400, then in development. Based on its original performance projections, this was significantly better than the 1986-vintage A340, which could claim only a 4 percent direct operating cost/seat reduction compared to the MD-11 on a 6,000 nautical mile flight.

Airbus's operating cost calculations were based on approximate selling prices of $84 million for the A340-300, $80 million for the A340-200, $85 million for the MD-11, $77.5 million for the MD-11ER, and $120 million for the 747-400.

The figures made a lot of sense to Lufthansa, which announced, on January 15, 1987, that its supervisory board had approved the purchase of 15 SuperFan-powered A340s,

To reduce pavement loading, the heavier A340 was designed with a center main undercarriage leg. The twin-wheel unit, built by Dowty Canada, was designed without brakes to reduce cost, weight, and maintenance costs. The same housing area was used as a fuel tank by the later A330-200 variant.

plus 15 options. Airbus was jubilant and hoped the deal would prompt the partner governments into supplying the launch aid loans to finally get the program going. Speaking at the rollout of the A320 on February 14, just a month later, French Prime Minister Jacques Chirac said, ". . . on the subject of the A330 and A340, I have already said that I hope France—or more exactly, Europe,—will not pass over what I believe to be a quite historic opportunity that is unlikely to be repeated for another 20 years, to take its rightful place in the long-haul market and thus benefit all airlines worldwide who have an interest in not sustaining a monopoly indefinitely."

Even as Chirac was voicing the European cause, an angry U.S. government delegation of fact finders arrived to begin a new round of talks with the four Airbus partners and their governments. Sparked by the deal with Lufthansa, and angered by the failure of any collaborative talks with MDC, the powerful political lobbyists of the American aerospace industry had forced their government into action. The Americans complained the A330/340 program would not be viable without massive launch subsidies from the British, French, and German governments. In line with previous complaints over the A300 and A320, it argued that such subsidies might be in breach of the General Agreement on Tariffs and Trade (GATT) rules.

The Europeans countered this claim by arguing that the U.S. industry benefited from "hidden" subsidies in the form of defense and research contracts, particularly through agencies such as NASA and government propulsion initiatives such as Integrated High Performance Turbine Engine Technology

Using the original A300 cross-section for an aircraft designed for much longer routes demanded innovative solutions when it came to crew-rest facilities. Working with what was then MBB, Airbus devised a compartment that could be housed in an L6-sized container and loaded into the belly of the aircraft when needed. The compartment has five bunks, a changing room, a refrigerator, and an entertainment system, and could be reached by steps from an entrance on the main deck. *Airbus*

The original A340 wing design, incorporating variable camber technology, is shown in this November 1986 impression. Within months, the design would be altered significantly to compensate for the loss of the SuperFan engine option and to deliver the performance promises made at the time. *Airbus*

(IHPTET). Ironically, the U.S. intervention had the opposite effect and actually stiffened the resolve of the hitherto luke-warm British government to support the program.

On March 12 the A330, by now designated the –200, received its first commitments when Air France Europe (Air Inter) signed for 5 firm and 15 options, and Thai Airways International for four firm and 4 options (later increased to 8). The following day, feeling full of renewed confidence, the consortium announced, ". . . so far, Airbus Industrie has obtained 104 commitments from 9 customers for both aircraft versions. Therefore, the supervisory board has decided to take all necessary steps for a formal launch decision by mid-April 1987 to ensure first deliveries of the A340 in May 1992, to be followed by first deliveries of the A330 a year later."

Sure enough, a second A340 commitment came on March 31, 1987, when Northwest Airlines signed a letter of intent for 20 A340s and options on 10 A330s. An engine selection was not announced at the time for the A340s, but Northwest planned to sign for the SuperFan on April 3.

It was then that events took a bizarre and, to Airbus, disastrous turn. On April 7 the aviation world and Airbus were stunned by a shock announcement from IAE that it would not be building the SuperFan.

Bouncing Back

Airbus reeled from the shock of the IAE announcement, but immediately contacted CFMI for a solution (see chapter

3). The very next day, on April 8, the two signed an agreement covering the use of the redesigned CFM56-5C1 engine on the aircraft.

But Airbus knew engine changes would not be enough to deliver the same performance as it had promised to the airlines. In frantic haste Airbus set about yet another redesign to recapture what it could of the SuperFan specification A340. This it achieved by increasing the wingspan from 183 feet 9 inches to 192 feet 3 inches, and replacing the A310-style wing tip fences with 9 foot 6 inch tall winglets. The same changes were also adopted by default for the A330. Together with the improved thrust promised by CFMI, Airbus hoped the A340 would come close to its earlier predictions.

Maximum takeoff weight of both A340 versions was increased by 17,600 pounds to 542,300 pounds, while payload-range for the –200 reduced slightly to 7,700 nautical miles with 262 passengers. The –300 range with 295 passengers similarly fell slightly to 6,850 nautical miles. Orders and commitments at this point included 87 for the A340 and 41 for the A330, but the SuperFan fiasco had caused the firm launch date to slip until at least May.

This, of course, depended ultimately on securing government launch aid and, surprisingly given the British government's uneven Airbus track record, it was the United Kingdom that became the first of the three to sanction state aid. Just before the British Parliament was dissolved for the summer

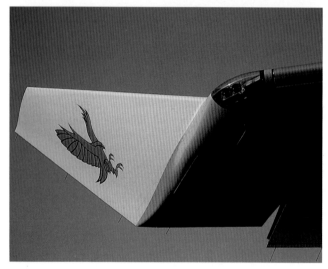

To scrape back performance effectively lost with the SuperFan, the wing was augmented with large composite winglets. First unveiled around April 1987, the winglet design was slender and sharply raked. By September 1989, the design was broader in chord than first envisaged, covering approximately 90 percent of the wing tip chord. The device measures just over 6 feet in length and is canted out by 42.5 degrees from the vertical. Span increased from 192 feet 5 inches to 197 feet 10 inches as a result, and wing area grew from 3,892 square feet to 3,908 square feet.

recess that May, Geoffrey Pattie, minister of state for industry, announced funding of £450 million. It was a long way short of the £750 million originally requested by BAe, but the company gladly accepted the aid, particularly as the repayment terms and conditions were greatly improved in the revised deal. As in previous Airbus loans, the government money was repayable on a fixed time scale at an agreed fixed rate of interest, but mainly through funds generated by a levy on the aircraft sold—starting with a specific aircraft down the line.

In France, Aerospatiale agreed to a repayable advance of 90 percent on its share of the $1.7 billion development costs. The German government, for its part, had originally set up DM 3.1 billion ($1.7 billion) of credit to support the Airbus initiative across all programs. By the time the A330/A340 appeared, some DM 2.9 billion of this had been used up, and Bonn was forced to extend the credit.

Attempts to reduce the level of government support for Airbus were strongly resisted by Franz-Josef Strauss. Apart from being a leading light in Airbus and the president of Deutsche Airbus, Strauss was also the premier of Bavaria and a partner in the crucial center-right coalition that held sway over the future of the government in the run-up to the election that year. However, when the German support package was finally cleared in the first few days of June that year, it contained an addendum that surprisingly called for the revival of collaborative talks with MDC.

By this time Airbus had also entered into an agreement with Fiat Aviazone of Italy covering a 4 percent share in the new program. A similar agreement, including some research work, was also concluded the following month with five Australian companies: Aerospace Technologies, British Aerospace (Australia), Dunlop Aviation, Hawker de Havilland, and Lucas Aerospace. All deals were cut on the basis of a production run of at least 800 aircraft.

At last, with the 1987 Paris air show only days away, and funding secured from all major government partners, Airbus was in a comfortable position to give the formal go-ahead to the A330 and A340. On June 5, it announced the launch of the program on the back of commitments for 130 aircraft from 10 airlines. The tally included orders for 89 A340s and 41 A330s from Lufthansa, Northwest, Air France, Air Inter, Thai Airways International, and International Lease Finance Company (ILFC), the innovative California-based lessor.

Paris provided the showcase opportunity for Lufthansa to sign a deal reconfirming its original A340-

Lufthansa led the pack by signing the first definitive agreement to buy the A340 at the 1987 Paris air show, having signaled its intention to purchase up to 30 earlier that year. Just 12 years later, in May 1999, Lufthansa took delivery of the 2,000th Airbus aircraft ever built when it accepted 1 of 49 A340s ordered since the start of the program.

200 purchase commitment. The deal, this time with CFM56 engines, was reportedly worth some $2.5 billion for all 30 aircraft, and the airline chairman, Reinhardt Abraham, stressed it was not getting the A340 at a "give-away price." Although Abraham admitted the CFM-powered version would burn more fuel than the SuperFan version, he said maintenance costs would be lower and direct operating costs would be, "within 1 percent" of the original SuperFan goals.

Formal launch ensured the two aircraft would have a fighting chance of being on time for their planned certification target dates of May 1992 for the A340, and first quarter 1993 for the A330. Airbus also updated its forecast for the big jetliners, and estimated a combined total of 1,000 split evenly between the two.

Airbus reflected on its good fortune at the show. After more than 15 years of planning, 18 months of argument, and several false starts, the consortium had finally launched its next two family members. Although at times it seemed the program would be aborted, and had been through several protracted time-wasting sessions while the collaborative venture with MDC was being explored, the omens now looked much better. It had even staved off the considerable threat posed by the brilliantly stage-managed launch of the MD-11, surviving the onslaught with the not inconsiderable loss of a key potential A340 user, Swissair. Then, to add insult to injury, it had undergone the extraordinary SuperFan affair that not only wasted time but had caused embarrassment to all concerned.

Now all Airbus had to do was to go and build them!

33

CHAPTER THREE
POWERFUL MOVERS

By the early 1980s, new four-engined airliner programs were virtually nonexistent. This was in part due to the influence of Airbus and its pioneering development of the A300, the world's first wide-body twin. Every subsequent western-built jetliner, with the exception of the small four-engined Hawker-Siddeley (later British Aerospace) 146, was either a twin or trijet.

International Aero Engines based its SuperFan concept on the core of the V2500 and its promising foothold at Airbus on the A320 family. Here in this artist's rendering, the futuristic engine is shown mounted on the A340-300, a new stretched variant that was only made possible by the advent of the 30,000-pound thrust SuperFan.

It was with some excitement, therefore, that all the engine makers watched Airbus finalize its plans for the four-engined TA11. From the beginning of this study in its A300B11 guise, the jetliner had been provisionally base-lined with the CFM International CFM56 that saw its first large-scale commercial success on the McDonnell Douglas DC-8 reengining program in 1979.

Ironically, it has been argued that the launch of the DC-8 Series 70, as the CFM56-powered versions were called, delayed the go-ahead of what would eventually become the A340. In reality, the impact of the DC-8 Series 70 on the

global airliner market was negligible in the long term, and any delay only helped benefit the final design of both the engine for the A340 as well as the airframe itself.

As far as CFM was concerned, the main threat on the TA11 was not so much the prospect of interminable delays, but that the bigger engine makers Rolls-Royce (R-R) and Pratt & Whitney (P&W) would come in with competing power-plants of their own. Indeed Airbus studied various trijet configurations of the TA11 with RB211-535s or JT10D-232s. Although these came to nothing, the option of larger engines was a constant worry to CFM.

By 1983, the threat emerged once more as both R-R and P&W offered de-rated versions of the RB211-535 and the successor of the JT10 effort, in the PW2000. The TA11 was offered with two fuselage lengths, seating either 230 or 270 passengers, but Airbus was wary of being wooed by the larger engines into making the aircraft too large.

In something of a coup, CFM worked hard to persuade Airbus that it was better to base the design around four engines already matched for the 27,500-pound to 30,000-pound thrust range, rather than operate bigger and more expensive engines at a de-rated setting. Although it was a strong temptation for Airbus to have the extra power up its sleeve for future growth, Airbus was keen to avoid overdesigning the aircraft and penalize operators by carrying around unnecessary structural weight.

Previous Page: Provisionally baselined by Airbus from the start of the A300B11 studies through the early 1970s onwards, the CFM56 was gradually increased in size to match the evolving A340 design. Competition from IAE's SuperFan concept eventually forced CFM to raise the engine's fan diameter to 72.3 inches from the 68 inch size originally conceived. Ironically Lufthansa, launch customer for the A340, chose the SuperFan but was forced to equip with the CFM56 when the IAE engine project was scrapped.

In its short life, the design of the SuperFan went through considerable evolution. Booster, or low-pressure compressor, stages were originally mounted in front of the variable-pitch fan (left), but later migrated to a more conventional position behind the fan (right). At the heart of the engine lay a 3:1 reduction gearbox that drove a set of 16 hollow-titanium fan blades. Bypass ratio was set at 17.5:1 and fan diameter was almost 9 feet.

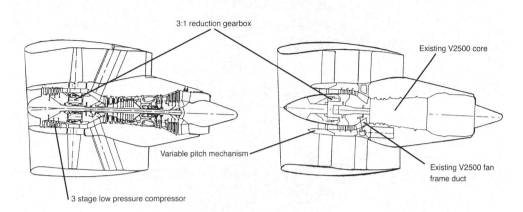

3:1 reduction gearbox

Existing V2500 core

Variable pitch mechanism

Existing V2500 fan frame duct

3 stage low pressure compressor

Airbus was further convinced by arguments from CFM's fledgling competitor, International Aero Engines (IAE). This joint company, formed in 1983, combined the strengths of P&W, R-R, Fiat, MTU, and several Japanese aerospace companies. It was created to develop an engine called the V2500 to compete with the CFM56 for a host of new technology twins then on the drawing board in Europe and the United States. International Aero Engines had arisen from the ashes of

CFMI's crucial link to Airbus was built through the CFM56-5A1 engine on the A320, which made its maiden flight in February 1987. The relationship with Airbus, though severely strained at times, has prospered over the years and is set to move to new heights through the application of advanced propulsion features developed through CFM's Tech56 program.

General Electric gained pole position on the A330/A340 through its enormous influence on the CFM56, developed in partnership with SNECMA. GE's willingness to support CFM's redesign of the CFM56 to meet the A340's performance promises in 1987 effectively rescued the program after the SuperFan fiasco. The result was the picture on the right—CFM56s exclusively on the A340, and CF6-80E1s first to be offered on the A330-300.

several other smaller engine projects, notably the Rolls-Royce RJ500, all of which had failed to clinch market interest. The chief loss, and the moment that led to the birth of IAE, had come in March 1981 when two American airlines, USAir and Southwest Airlines, had ordered the new Boeing 737-300 with the CFM56 engine. This move created the legendary relationship between CFMI and the 737, and would make IAE desperate for business.

The real battle to power the TA11 began in the two years leading up to the formal go-ahead of the A340 in 1986. In 1984 both the CFM56 and V2500-powered versions of the A320 were launched, providing a crucial opportunity for Airbus to work closely with both engine makers. Airbus saw how each coped with the various challenges of fitting their engines to the new twin.

Through 1986, CFMI and IAE worked hard with Airbus to agree on the thrust requirements for the A340. In October, it was CFMI that won the initial breakthrough when it signed

a memorandum of understanding with Airbus to develop a "throttle push" version of the CFM56-5A1, dubbed the –5S2, and rated at 28,600 pounds thrust. The –5A1 was the engine developed for the A320, and CFMI planned to milk the advantage of commonality for all it was worth.

"The commonality with the CFM56-5A1 engine on the A320 will offer airlines unique investment savings," said

With spoilers up, slats out, flaps down, brakes on, and thrust reversers deployed, this Lufthansa-owned A340-300 Airbus demonstrator comes to a stop in a little over 2,000 feet of runway at the Farnborough show. Development of the four-door, target-type thrust reverser was made necessary by the use of a new, long-duct mixed-flow nacelle to optimize long-range cruise performance.

CFMI's marketing and advanced applications vice president at the time, Ron Welsch. The agreement called for four engines to be delivered in June 1990 for the first A340 flight test aircraft, with a maiden flight expected in the first quarter of 1991. Certification of the –5S2 was set for 1990, and aircraft certification for 1992.

Then, just when it appeared everything was cast in stone, along came IAE with the V2500 SuperFan.

Up to this stage, IAE had been outflanked by CFMI. The Franco-U.S. company had successfully established itself on the A340, leaving IAE out in the cold. International Aero Engine's only real advantage in the battle so far had been its technology. With no market to compare to its longer established rival, IAE desperately applied leading edge technology wherever possible in order to attract business. It tried every innovation, including titanium rotors, blades, and casings to achieve better performance. While the promises of better performance helped attract valuable customers, such as its 1994 launch order from Pan American on the A320, it also meant inevitable development challenges. These culminated in terrible "melt-down" problems with the high-pressure compressor and, at one point, cast serious doubts over the entire survival of the whole program.

It was against this background, therefore, that IAE attempted to break CFMI's hold on the A340. At the time, IAE's best offering was the 27,500-pound thrust development of the V2500-A1. Both Airbus and IAE knew this was insufficient thrust for the new quad jet, even though it was not far below the thrust promised at the time by CFMI.

International Aero Engine was left with no choice. If there was to be any chance of getting a place on the A340 it had to come up with something radically new. The answer was a revolutionary concept in which the fan was driven by a core-mounted gear system. This was IAE's fabled "SuperFan."

The proposed engine featured a large, ducted fan and offered a substantial increase in thrust, to over 30,000 pounds, as well as dramatically reduced fuel consumption. International Aero Engine told an astonished Airbus that the engine would have a specific fuel consumption 8 percent to 17 percent lower than the baseline V2500, which was itself already noticeably more fuel efficient than the CFM56.

These promises were too good to ignore and, for Airbus, the SuperFan changed everything. Now Airbus had an engine with which its new aircraft could outperform its closest rival, the planned McDonnell Douglas MD-11. Like the early signs

Generating up to 72,000 pounds of thrust, the twin-shaft General Electric CF6-80E1 turbofan relies heavily on its massive fan blades to pump air flow at up to 1,913 pounds per second! The engine's high bypass ratio of 5.3 contributes to low noise levels and a cruise fuel burn rate of a little over half a pound of fuel, per pound force, per hour. SNECMA produces around 20 percent of the A330 engine in terms of total volume production.

of a terrible storm, the forecast performance of the U.S. trijet already showed it would easily beat the A340 in terms of payload and range. Worse still, the choice of the –5S2 meant that, from the outset, there was virtually no room for growth.

Armed with the SuperFan option, Airbus went back to the drawing board. Throughout 1986 the A340 was redefined into two basic options: a 262-seat –200 with a range of 7,850 nautical miles; and a 4.3m stretched version, the –300, capable of carrying 295 passengers over 7,000 nautical miles.

Almost overnight, the new-look A340 began attracting interest from airlines and, within weeks of the redesign, Lufthansa became the first to commit to the A340 on January 15, 1987. Significantly, Lufthansa chose the SuperFan to power the 30 aircraft it ordered, and most industry observers expected Northwest, which was also in final negotiations for up to 30 more A340s, to follow suit.

However, everyone, including Airbus, was in for a shock. Northwest signed a letter of intent for the A340, but no engine was specified. At this stage, this was something of a surprise given the apparent performance advantage over the CFM56 promised by the SuperFan. Rumors began circulat-

ing around the industry that Northwest had uncovered hints of trouble with the advanced new engine before it was even built.

Airbus, meanwhile, was apparently blissfully unaware of this new uncertainty and prepared to get going with the SuperFan. On April 7, 1987, an Airbus team headed by president Jean Pierson flew to P&W's headquarters in East Hartford. The team clutched attaché cases containing legal documents, and planned to sign a definitive agreement with IAE covering the development of the SuperFan and its application to the A340.

Instead, to the total shock of the Airbus team, P&W informed them that the SuperFan was effectively dead, and IAE had been premature in its offer to develop the engine! A dumbfounded Pierson was presented with a hurried alternative plan from P&W, which revived the previously abandoned option of fitting the PW2000 to the A340. Pierson's party left

The CF6-80E1-powered A330-300 entered service in January 1994, and a little over one year later the type earned 180-minute ETOPS approval. With a compressor ratio up to 34.6:1, the –80E1 was the ultimate variant of the CF6 family, which had originally grown from the TF39 engine developed in the 1960s to power the Lockheed C-5 Galaxy.

The 100-inch diameter fan PW4168 for the A330-300 was the first derivative growth model in Pratt & Whitney's PW4000 engine family. Rated at 64,000-pound and 68,000-pound thrust levels, the engine was theoretically capable of 75,000-pounds thrust if needed. Launched for the A330 in December 1991, it first flew on the big twin in October 1993 and entered service with Thai International Airways in December 1994. The PW4168-powered A330 was cleared for 180-minute ETOPS in July 1995.

the United States feeling an unfortunate blend of fury, disappointment, and panic. The SuperFan had clearly been a game changer but now it was gone; so what were they going to do?

The answer came from CFMI that never abandoned the chase for what it saw was its rightful position on the A340. The engine maker's charge was led by Brian Rowe, who, in 1980 as group executive in charge of GE Aircraft Engines, had pushed the risky decision to develop a cropped fan version of the CFM56 for the 737. Even Rowe, who is widely acclaimed as the father of the high bypass ratio turbofan through his pioneering work on the GE TF36/CF6, did not know his gutsy move would lead to the best-selling engine/airframe combination in jetliner history.

"Airbus was floundering around looking for an engine, so I gave Jean Pierson a ring and said: 'Look, we will agree to

build an engine with a bigger fan diameter.' So we cut a deal with Pierson on the A340 and made the French government very pleased because it saved the program," said Rowe, a straight-talking Englishman who had gained his early knowledge at R-R before emigrating to the United States.

The deal with Airbus had strings attached, however. It was linked to a proposed agreement giving GE sole-supplier status on the first 100 A330s, as well as an undertaking from Airbus that it would use the A variant of the new A340 engine on a stretched A320, should it be developed. Although the semi-exclusive deals never materialized in this form, CFMI and Airbus did sign an agreement on an "improved engine" for the A340, and at the same time GE and Airbus concluded a separate deal to develop an up-rated version of the CF6-80C2 for the A330.

A proposed growth version of the PW4000 was selected by US Airways for a new fleet of A330s, but the airline later reverted to standard PW4168s. The proposed 73,000-pound growth version, dubbed the PW4173, presented unexpectedly expensive technical challenges and was abandoned in 2000. Instead, P&W later began talks with Airbus over upgrading the existing A330 engines with advanced features like a low emissions TALON combustor.

The first thing to do was redesign the basic engine to pump more power so it could come close to the levels promised by the SuperFan. Without higher thrust the aircraft would not be able to perform the missions that Lufthansa and Northwest specified.

CFMI vice president at the time, Frank Homan, recalled the changes. "We decided 68 inches (fan diameter) was no longer adequate and we jumped to 72.3 inches. We were facing the SuperFan and we explained that fundamental reliability hinges on the core. We had enjoyed outstanding reliability of the –3 and the –5, and what Airbus was buying in our offering was the prospect of a very reliable machine from the word go, versus a paper offering with potential problems. We also predicted that the net performance delta was not as large

as they promised because, although the specific fuel consumption of a very high bypass ratio engine is lower, the installed drag is higher."

The SuperFan fiasco, as it later became known, certainly stimulated the A340 program in unexpected directions, though CFMI's decision to grow the CFM56 would have probably come sooner or later, said Homan. "It was not exactly rocket science. We had done studies to see what could be done and we felt the engine had it in it to grow. There were no great decisions as to whether we should do it or not. The aircraft needed it and we went ahead and did it."

In spite of the decision to extend the fan, CFMI opted to retain the mid-span shroud first introduced on the CFM56-3 version powering the 737. Although wide-chord fan blades were becoming increasingly popular, CFMI saw no benefit in risking the expense of such a development for the –5C version, as the A340 engine was called. In fact, it would not be until the launch of the next-generation 737 in 1993 that CFMI would develop a version of the CFM56 with this feature.

In tests, the –5C demonstrated fan efficiency (measured from forward of the fan to aft of the outlet guide vanes) of greater than 0.91. "This is better than any other unshrouded fan," claimed Jacques Rossignol, who was then SNECMA technical director and would later be president of CFMI. As blade diameters increased, engine makers devised mid-span shrouds (clappers or snubbers as they are sometimes called), to help improve airflow through the fan as well as provide structural support. The tinkling, metallic sound often heard coming from jet engines windmilling while at rest at airport gates is generally caused by the shrouds gently tapping against each other as the fan slowly rotates.

Further downstream in the engine one of the biggest changes to the –5C was in the four-stage low-pressure (LP) compressor. As well as having one extra stage to help increase overall pressure ratio, the dovetail blade roots previously used were replaced with a groove running around the disc into which the blades were slotted to save costs.

CFMI also took advantage of the –5C redesign to build in new features to combat serious "flame out" problems that it had encountered with its earlier engines. On the 737 in particular, this had manifested itself when flying through severe hail and rainstorms, and in one case in 1988 had led to a 737-300 making an emergency landing with both engines failed, on a narrow grass strip beside a Louisiana bayou. To ensure that water and hail was not ingested into the core of the engine, the –5C fan/core splitter plate was moved aft. Water was therefore centrifuged outwards into the bypass duct, rather than sucked through the heart of the engine.

To reduce hail ingestion, a shallow scoop was also added in the duct outer wall between the LP and high-pressure (HP) compressors to dump hail overboard through variable bypass valves.

The HP compressor was essentially unchanged from the –3 and the –5A design, but incorporated a new fourth-stage bleed design. As in the –5A, developed for the A320, an extra roller bearing behind the main thrust bearing helped to center the core. The revised aerodynamics of the –5C core were later made available as a retrofit kit for the –5A.

Rolls-Royce's Trent 700 is characterized by 26 wide-chord fan blades measuring 97.4 inches in diameter. The U.K. manufacturer introduced the world's first wide chord blades on the RB.211-535E4 engine for the Boeing 757 and gradually introduced the concept on virtually every subsequent powerplant. The titanium blades are hollow, and twisted to pump the maximum amount of air. They also have a reputation for coping well with bird strikes; the similar shaped blades on a 757 are known to have survived an encounter with a flock of Canada geese on takeoff from Chicago. The engine chopped its way through at least four 7-pound birds and ran long enough to help get the aircraft around the circuit and back for a safe landing.

The combustor was also basically unchanged and staged combustion was used to reduce emissions, a growing need in the increasingly environmentally conscious European arena. In staged burning, only half of the fuel injectors were used. This helped cut emissions of nitrogen oxides to levels more than 40 percent below International Civil Aviation Organization recommended amounts. To ensure the engine ran efficiently at all times, and thus further help reduce unnecessary emissions, it was fitted with a full-authority digital engine control (FADEC). Although this derived from the –5A controller, it was loaded with new control law software and new electronics. The FADEC provided active clearance control of the HP compressor and LP and HP turbines. Active clearance meant that cooling air was switched by the FADEC to either the casing or the rotating stages as needed to ensure a tight fit between the blades and the walls of the compressor and turbine stages. This meant continued high efficiency, while minimizing the chances of an expensive "rub" between a blade tip and the casing itself.

The single stage HP turbine was unchanged from the –5A, including the use of single-crystal, high-temperature resistant blades. The LP turbine was completely redesigned, however, with a fifth stage added to drive the bigger fan.

The –5C was also the first CFM56 with a mixed-flow nacelle in which the core and bypass air was mixed internally, within the aft part of the nacelle itself, rather than exiting and mixing in the free air-stream behind the engine. It was the first use of forced mixing on any CFM56, and in-flight tests showed 80 percent mixing effectiveness. The duct was designed by San Diego-based Rohr (later part of the renamed Goodrich Corporation), and equipped with an unusual four-door thrust-reverser built by Hispano. CFMI supplied the entire "propulsion system" complete with engine, nacelle, thrust reverser, and systems directly to Airbus as a finished product. The complete powerplant weighed in about 400 pounds heavier than any previous CFM56.

The plan called for engine tests to begin in the last quarter of 1989. The engine was to be rated (as the –5C3) at 32,500 pounds thrust, with initial service rating (as the –5C2) at 31,200 pounds thrust following certification in October 1991. Flight testing was expected to start on GE's 707 test bed at Mojave, California, in May 1990, with the first flight on the A340 itself scheduled for the following April.

By the end of November 1989, plans were finalized for a 100-hour test program at SNECMA's Villaroche site in France, to be followed by a further test phase at GE's Peebles facility in Ohio. In all, the company expected more than 5,000 hours of tests, which began with the first ground-runs on December 27. The slightly late start, caused by last-minute adjustments to the larger fan, also caused a knock-on effect to the first flight of the engine that took place on August 29, 1990, three months later than originally planned.

Testing began well, however, and the engine reached its top initial thrust rating of 31,200 pounds on the first flight. As flight tests continued, CFMI and Airbus worked on plans for the first significant growth model, the –5C4. These were finalized the following December when the two signed an agreement to develop the 34,000 pounds thrust version.

Compared to the –5C3 version, which was a simple adjustment to the FADEC, the –5C4 incorporated several modifications to boost thrust. The fan hub was modified to reduce exhaust gas temperatures and raise the LP compressor pressure ratio. New temperature resistant materials were also used in the HP and LP turbine blades and vanes to further help raise the thrust capability.

Finally, with tests completed, the first shipset of engines was dispatched to Toulouse for installation on the prototype A340, a –300. Engine run-ups and systems were undertaken throughout the late summer and, with winter on the way, the four CFM56-5C2s powered the prototype into the air for the first time on October 25, 1991.

Twins Times Three

While the industry watched enthralled as the SuperFan fiasco played itself out, the engine story for the A330 was routine by comparison.

Given the events surrounding CFMI's effective "rescue" of the A340 in 1987, it came as no surprise when later that year a higher thrust variant of GE's CF6-80C2 was the first to be offered on the big twin. In 1988, Airbus signed agreements with R-R and P&W for the use of new high thrust versions of the RB.211-524L and PW4164 respectively.

The agreements marked historic milestones for all concerned. It was the first time engines from all of the Big Three powerplant giants had been offered on a single Airbus aircraft, and the first use of a R-R engine on any Airbus.

Almost immediately it seemed GE had the advantage. Not only was it the first off the mark with an agreement with Airbus, it also offered the largest diameter fan and the biggest core. This translated into higher thrust and better overall

A peek up the business end of the Trent 700's exhaust pipe reveals the aft section of the four-stage low-pressure turbine, the bypass duct, and the bypass duct outlet guide vanes. Note the heat-affected coloring of the titanium material making up the exhaust duct, tail cone, and the underside of the pylon attachment.

performance, particularly during takeoff in a twin when every ounce of power becomes crucial in case of a single engine failure.

Although early specifications for the A330 suggested a requirement for engines in the 60,000-pound to 65,000-pound thrust range, it quickly became obvious to GE that more power would be needed. General Electric therefore set about growing the 93 inch diameter fan of the –80C2 variant to 96 inches for the new version, which it called the CF6-80E1.

The aerodynamics of the individual fan blades was also improved with a change to the camber. The slightly wider blades took up more room, so their numbers were reduced from 38 to 34 in the new engine that was sized to deliver between 63,000 pounds and almost 70,000 pounds of thrust. To cope with the higher thrust, the flow capacity of the LP compressor was increased by 9 percent, while pressure ratio was boosted by 12 percent.

The basic geometry of the 14-stage HP compressor was unchanged from the –80C2, but GE introduced high-temperature alloys into the last stage to handle the tougher thermal environment of the more powerful engine. Overall pressure ratio of the HP compressor was increased from 30.4 in the –80C2 to 32.6 in the first versions of the E1, and as high as 34.6 in the 69,500-pound thrust –80E1A3.

New high-temperature alloys and improved cooling systems were also introduced into both the LP and HP turbines. The march of microelectronic technology also allowed GE to design in an on-wing programmable FADEC with the capability to control a higher capacity fuel system.

The big engine weighed in at almost 11,200 pounds without fuel and oil sloshing around its insides, and at almost 15,000 pounds by the time the nacelle and reverser were attached. The improvements paid off, however, and on its first run in December 1990, the E1 generated an impressive 72,000 pounds thrust.

Pratt & Whitney meanwhile signed its agreement with Airbus in July 1988. It originally discussed a 64,000-pound thrust version of the popular PW4000 family dubbed the PW4164, but, like GE, found the thrust requirement growing. The agreement, therefore, covered the development of the 68,000 pound thrust PW4168 for certification in mid-1992.

Like its erstwhile competitor, P&W also increased fan diameter to boost thrust. The 38-blade fan grew from 93.6

The inward "toeing" of the Trent engines is evident as this Cathay Pacific Airways A330-300 noses toward the camera in 1997. The first Trent 768-powered A330 was delivered to Cathay on February 27, 1995, with 90-minutes ETOPS approval already in hand. Further extensions to the ETOPS approval limits to 120 and 180 minutes were given in 1996.

inches on the baseline engine, powering the A300, A310, and Boeing 767, to 99.8 inches. An additional stage was added to the standard four-stage LP compressor, while an extra LP turbine stage was also added to the existing four-stage unit. High-performance turbine capability was increased by changes to the internal cooling design. Overall bypass ratio was 5.1, while fan pressure ratio rose to a worthy 1.75.

The extra stages and larger diameter fan resulted in a longer engine that ended in a new mixed-flow exhaust design and a longer duct. Both features were expected to result in lower noise levels, an increasingly important marketing aspect.

Pratt & Whitney's mighty PW4168, and its de-rated PW4164 spin-off variant, weighed 14,350 pounds.

While GE and P&W fell into a familiar routine of developing new variants for yet another Airbus twin, it was all new territory for R-R. Since pre-Airbus days the U.K. engine maker had struggled to get aboard the increasingly successful European enterprise. It had come closest with the V2500 on the A320 through its IAE membership, but had otherwise been left out in the cold despite being baseline on five of the six twin-aisle precursors to the A300. Various engines had been proposed ranging from the RB.178 (an early conceptual competitor to the JT9D), the RB.207, a study engine alternative to the CF6-50, and even the Spey 50.

Now, as the competition for the A330 loomed, R-R had a far more successful pedigree on which to base its bid—the vastly improved RB.211-524 and the smaller –535E4. The latter engine, which was offered on the Boeing 757 in competition with P&W's PW2000, enjoyed more than 60 percent of the market and showed the U.K. engine maker could do well if it was allowed to compete. There, however, lay the problem. Rolls-Royce was available on a relatively limited number of types and, as a result, the company had only 8 percent of the world market in 1987.

The company therefore followed a conscious strategy to widen the product line. At the lower end of the thrust range it joined forces with Williams in the United States, and BMW in Germany. At the top end, it sharpened pencils and cleared computer screens to develop a new engine family for the next generation of wide-bodies that Airbus, Boeing, and McDonnell Douglas were planning. The new engine family was to be called the Trent, and would be aimed at every new application.

The Trent was based heavily on the original triple-shaft concept pioneered with the first RB.211 design for the Lockheed TriStar, and in its early form for the A330 was known to Airbus until 1989 as the R.211-524L. Although strongly critical of the design, even R-R's fierce competitors acknowledged that the inherently heavy triple-shaft concept would begin to show advantages as the thrust requirement increased.

It was with this in mind that R-R sketched out a common engine for both the MD-11 and the A330 in 1988. Dubbed the Trent 600, because it was aimed generically at the 60,000-pound thrust bracket, the engine was originally configured with a 2.41m diameter fan. The size was smaller than ideal for the A330, mainly to keep it within the narrow confines of the MD-11's "banjo fitting" in the tail engine position.

With the growth of the A330 thrust requirement, however, all this changed. Rolls-Royce could no longer meet the need and still maintain fan size commonality with the trijet. In addition, the engine maker saw the climb-thrust requirement of the twin was different, so the fan size was increased to 97.5 inches, and the whole Trent design optimized around the A330. The higher thrust level of 70,000 pounds also called for a new title, the Trent 700.

Focusing on the A330 was to prove a fortunate decision, since R-R failed to sell the Trent 600 on the MD-11, apart

from one order from Air Europe which later went bankrupt. In the longer run, the MD-11 itself was to suffer at the hands of both the A340 and the soon-to-be-launched 777, and deliveries finally ceased in 2001 with the 200th aircraft following Boeing's takeover of MDC in 1997. Rolls-Royce was able to focus its energies on the Trent 700, and later the 800. This latter engine would go on to clinch a greater share of the 777 market than any R-R had seen before on a Boeing wide-body.

The Trent followed the –535E4 in using wide-chord fan blades. Since its early and disastrous experience with composite blades on the early RB.211 (which badly delaminated in tests and contributed directly to the financial ruin of the company in the early 1970s), the company stuck with titanium for all of its new blade designs.

The Trent blades were made using a new technique called superplastic formed diffusion bonding in which three layers of titanium were laid upon each other and heated to the point where they could be molded and formed. The outside edges of the titanium sheets were bonded and an inert gas was then pumped into it to inflate the resulting envelope. An internal zigzag shaped stiffener added strength to the finished product.

The other key to the Trent 700 design was the eight-stage intermediate pressure (IP) compressor. In its two-shaft competitors, the heart of the engine lay in the HP compressor, but in the Trent it was the IP compressor. Rolls-Royce described it as "the supercharger, running at the optimum speed, that controls how much horsepower you get out of the core."

The engine also featured new high-temperature resistant single-crystal (CMSX-4) materials in both the single-stage HP turbine that drives the compressor, and the IP turbine. Extensive use was also made of three-dimensionally shaped blades to take advantage of analyzed differences in temperature and pressure distributions. This was particularly evident in the LP turbine that was sculpted into such a highly curved profile it looked more like a banana than a blade. The turbine on the Trent 700 contained four-stages, rather than the RB.211's three and the five used on the larger Trent 800.

By June 1992, the first Trent 700s were mounted in test cells for the start of the most exhausting evaluation in R-R history. Although it would be another two years before it became the first British engine to power an Airbus (see chapter 6), R-R soon got the feeling that it was onto a winner. Little could it guess at the time just how successful the future relationship between Airbus and the Trent family would become.

CHAPTER FOUR

BUILDING THE BIG JETS

The usual frantic pace set by the 1987 Paris air show was a suitable taste of things to come for the A330/A340 development team that summer. With firm launch approved, the clock was ticking.

Although essentially identical to the A330 wing, the A340 wing is strengthened around the outer engine pylon area, and the leading edge slats 4 and 5 are modified to accommodate the outer engine. Note the exceptional ground clearance of the outer engines in this head-on view of an Air Madagascar aircraft pictured at London Heathrow.

One of the most vital areas of airframe development for the new pair was the wing. By August 1987 the design teams in the United Kingdom had almost completed overall design, having launched into the final design phase the previous April. The wing, measuring more than 197 feet in span across the winglets, was the largest ever built in Europe and the most advanced.

It had the highest sweep of any Airbus to date, with a 30-degree angle, and although it had virtually the same span as the 747-200, it had only 65 percent of the area. The higher aspect ratio was selected to reduce takeoff and cruise drag. The most critical feature, and the most unique, was that the same wing could be used for both the twin A330 and the quad A340.

The secret behind this difficult achievement lay in the neat balance of bending moments exerted on the fuselage by the wing, between the twin- and four-engined versions. Engineers calculated the A330 and A340 bending moments were within 1.5 percent of each other, allowing the two structures to be assembled in the same jigs.

Previous Page: The basic cross-section of the A330/A340 fuselage was taken directly from the original A300 design. The main passenger cabin measures 208.2 inches wide at seat bottom level, while the fuselage itself measures 222 inches exactly outer wall to outer wall. Height to the overhead baggage compartments, when installed, was designed originally to be 65.7 inches, with aisle height to ceiling at 91.7 inches. Later interior changes were adopted on the A340-500/600 to increase spaciousness.

Because of bending relief from the weight of its outboard engines, the bending moment of a four-engined aircraft is substantially lower than it is for a twin at the same maximum takeoff weight. For the same fuselage weight, therefore, a twin needs a stronger, heavier wing than a quad. It follows that, for the same wing, the payload carried in the fuselage must be less for a twin than a four, which is exactly what happened with the A330/A340.

The A340 was designed to carry around 20 percent more payload, which translated into about 66,000 pounds of extra

The deep wing of the A310 provides the aerodynamic heritage for the A330/A340 wing, while its structural roots lay in the A300. The greater span of the new jetliner meant aspect ratio was set higher at 9.3, against 8.8 for the A310—an example of which is pictured on finals to land.

fuel, giving it longer range and the requirement for a center undercarriage leg. However, despite these vastly different characteristics, the A340 wing required a design strength only 1 percent higher than the A330.

The wing closely followed the structural blueprint established by the A300, and even included the inboard center spar (omitted on the A310 and A320), to support the extra large structure and provide extra damage tolerance. The center spar terminated outboard of the inboard engine. The leading edge slats, trailing edge flaps, spoilers, and ailerons differed from previous Airbus designs mainly because of the position of the engines. The wing was designed with seven slats per side with a gap between the fourth and fifth to accommodate the outboard engine pylon and, for the A330, a gap between the first and second for the inboard engine.

The decision to go for a FBW flight control system also led to the development of split ailerons. The ailerons were designed to droop for takeoff and landing to provide a full-span trailing edge flap. The ailerons were also made to deflect upwards after touchdown to increase lift dumping and braking efficiency. The ailerons also provided wing bending moment relief during maneuvering by deflecting upwards when the inboard airbrake panels were deployed.

Aerodynamically, the wing was a direct relation of the A310, although adjustments for the longer range cruise meant that aspect ratio was higher, at 9.3 against the smaller aircraft's 8.8. One of the most difficult tasks was the design of the outer engine installation, which was made differently from the inner mounts (the same for the A330 and A340) after aerodynamic studies showed signs of a stiff penalty. The design team discovered the A330 pylon would have pushed the outer engine too far forward. The revised design kept the engine forward by around 1 foot 4 inches to preserve what BAe hoped would be perfect performance in the "crucial gully" between the nacelle and the lower wingskin. As it transpired flight tests would later show the need for substantial modifications in this area.

Like the other partners, BAE invested heavily on new facilities to cope specifically with the demands of the new project. A three-story technical center, with a 160,000-square foot floor area, was built at Filton near Bristol at a cost of £7 million to house the design team and their computers. At Chester, the main production site for the new wings near Manchester, an investment of £5 million was poured into the construction of a new 150,000-square foot facility linking the main plant to a machine tool unit. The increase in floor

Ailerons droop when the crew selects full flaps, and deflect 25 degrees upwards along with the spoilers on landing to help dump lift. A close look reveals the ailerons are split, with the outer section remaining centered at speeds over 200 knots.

area enabled BAe to commission a new production line in late 1989.

A full-scale wooden mockup of the wing was also built to check the accuracy of the computer-based design, as well as some good old-fashioned draftsmanship. Engineering models of wing systems were also made to check the location of wiring and plumbing, and a 10-foot deep swing pit was also dug to test operations of the landing gear.

The ungainly and bulbous A300-600ST (Super Transporter) Beluga replaced the Super Guppies by October 1997. Apart from regularly hauling large parts of Airbus aircraft between European assembly sites, the Belugas have been chartered to carry other large and unusual cargoes ranging from enormous works of art to sections of the International Space Station. Largest cargo in terms of volume is the A330/A340 rear fuselage sections, while the heaviest carried in its 24 feet 3 inch wide interior, are the A330/A340 wings.

While the expansion of the British sites was impressive, it was in France where the truly monumental changes were taking place. The greatest of these was Aerospatiale's $411 million (Fr 2.5 billion) investment in a massive new assembly plant at Colomiers, adjacent to the existing Airbus site at Toulouse-Blagnac airport in southwest France.

Construction began six months after the firm launch of the A330/A340 project, and by November 1988 the first 70-feet-high concrete pillars had been erected on the 124-acre site. The large building was named the Clement Ader assembly hall in honor of the French engineer who, in 1890, briefly hopped into the air with a steam-powered, bat-winged aircraft.

Hoping for much more success than this, Airbus designed the plant to produce up to seven aircraft per month using large subassemblies flown in by Super Guppy, and later the Beluga fleet, from all over Europe. The roof of the enormous facility, weighing around 8,500 tons, was supported on 15 trusses, each of which had a span of more than 295 feet. The assembly hall itself was 1,640 feet long, more than 655 feet wide, and 150 feet high.

The site was designed around a modular assembly concept based on three main assembly phases and the heavy use of robots. Several high-tech robotic devices were brought in to drill the 3,500 holes required for the wing/fuselage join, and for joining the forward and rear fuselage sections to the wing/center fuselage section. The wing-fuselage mating process was designed to take about 35 hours over three days. Once the "backbone" had been completed, it was lifted by traveling crane to the second main station, where the front and rear sections were attached in a cycle lasting about 12 hours.

Here other components, such as tail and landing gear, were attached. The aircraft was then towed to one of four cells for finishing and general system testing. This latter part was timed to last about nine days, after which the aircraft would proceed to another hall for further system and interior furnishing as well as engine installation.

The modular concept, developed by Aerospatiale, allowed mating and ground testing to be carried out in specific workstations, rather than being performed gradually as the aircraft moved along the line. This system allowed Airbus to reduce the number of stations from as many as eight for the A320 to four for the bigger jetliners, and reduced the chances of the line stopping or slowing due to shortages of parts or equipment on other parts of the line.

The heart of the wing structure is revealed in this view of an A340 unit under construction at the BAE Systems-owned Airbus U.K. wing manufacturing facility in Brough, North Wales. The main wing box is made up of the three spars visible in the picture. Overall the structure is identical to that of the A330 apart from minor strengthening around the outboard engine pylon and changes to the number 4 and 5 leading edge slats.

Wing to fuselage mating holes were drilled by eight robots. Four were set up on each side, controlling a total of 120 drills per aircraft. The "Kuka" robots were based on similar machines used in car assembly, and were like another four robots developed by Game Ingenierie of France to join the fuselage sections. Fasteners and sealant were applied manually in the wing join process, whereas the fuselage assembly machines injected sealant. The robots saved an estimated 20 percent on labor costs and 5 percent on time. Working in partnership with a worker inside the aircraft, the fuselage joining robots drilled a hole, injected the sealant, and put the rivet in place. The worker then formed the head on the rivet, before the robot moved on to drill the next hole.

Fuselage junctions were made using four "dollies" that ran on rails placed around the outside of the fuselage. These each had three heads, one to drill a hole, a second to apply sealant, and a third to locate the fastener. Altogether, there were about 12,000 holes per section, and according to Airbus calculations, the process saved 15 percent on labor costs.

Major investment was also undertaken at Aerospatiale's aircraft divisions at Saint-Nazaire, Meaulte, and Nantes. Construction began in early 1988 on a new assembly shop in Nantes for the top and bottom panels of the wingspar boxes. The site included two remotely controlled overhead conveyors and six fully automatic riveting machines, and an automatic bolting machine for mating the box panels.

Some Fr14 million was invested at the Meaulte site where two new automatic riveting machines were set up for the building of the A330/A340 door and lower forward fuselage sections. A further Fr21 million was allocated to setting up a "flexible" machining unit. As with previous Airbus programs, the Saint-Nazaire site was allocated responsibility for the manufacture of the center fuselage, although for the first time this was to include components supplied from outside France.

Saint-Nazaire was also vested with the task of joining the nose section to the forward fuselage made by Deutsche Airbus (MBB). The complete unit was then flown to the new Colomiers facility, rather than arriving at the final assembly line in separate components as with previous Airbus aircraft.

The first sheet metal parts for the A330/A340 were machined in Germany in July 1988. In the buildup to the launch of the program, MBB had invested DM400 million ($225 million) in new production facilities at six manufacturing sites on the Weser estuary. These included a specialized machining site at Varel, numerically controlled forming at

The Beluga's 123-foot cargo compartment can gulp down a set of fully equipped wings for the A330 or A340. It takes the Beluga 19 flying hours to transport all the components for one A340--a major improvement over the Super Guppy, which would have needed about 54 hours. After the conversion from the Super Guppy to the Beluga, Airbus was able to cut transport costs by a third.

Bremen, fuselage panels in Einswarden, and an interior fittings center in Hamburg. Germany had responsibility for the entire rear fuselage section.

This part, like the entire fuselage, was essentially little changed in detailed design from the original A300B2. The geometry, sketched around two standard LD3 cargo containers side by side, remained the same, as did the location of stringers, floor beams, and frames. It was mostly in the areas of materials and joining techniques where Airbus took advantage of the technical advances made over the intervening 15 years.

Fuselage construction followed standard Airbus practice: a conventional aluminum monocoque structure with sheet metal or, in some areas, machined frames and open-section sheet metal stringers. Fuselage skins were formed from sheet metal, except in highly loaded areas such as the side and lower center-fuselage panels where the skins were machined. Stringers were attached by hot bonding above the window line, and by conventional riveting below.

Other changes were made as a result of lessons learned from the explosion of a hand grenade in an aft lavatory on a Thai Airways International A300-600 several years before, as well as from the Sioux City DC-10 accident. Both had revealed the need for improved monitoring for stress and corrosion in the closed-off area aft of the rear pressure bulkhead, which was made more accessible from behind as a result.

Another unusual aspect of the fuselage design was how to accommodate the A340's center fuselage landing leg without compromising the common structure for the A330. The answer was to design a box-section keel beam that in the A330 is closed off with skin panels and in the A340 contained the undercarriage, doors, and local reinforcement.

The A340 also featured a center-section fuel tank that was available for later, longer-range A330 versions. In common with the A310-300, both aircraft also had a tail plane trim tank and a computerized fuel system that automatically adjusted the center-of-gravity position to minimize total drag and which was expected to save up to 1.5 percent in cruise fuel burn.

Another innovation was the introduction of a new hybrid carbon-fiber, glass-fiber reinforced plastic for the huge center section fairing, known to Airbus and its manufacturer Aerospatiale as the "bathtub." This formed a smooth aerodynamic fairing over the fuselage-wing join area and was nearly 74 feet long.

For the first time, Airbus also introduced significant amounts of aluminum-lithium into the airframe. The material was around 14 percent lighter than standard aircraft alloy, but its high manufacturing costs (up to four times as expensive as conventional aluminum) and doubts about its fatigue performance continued to delay its widespread use. Airbus held off from full-scale use on fuselage panels, and

Wings were originally mated to the fuselage in a cycle that took about 35 hours over three days, though Airbus later developed processes to reduce the time in periods of higher production demand. Overall production cycle time for the A340 had been reduced to 18 months in 1994 and to 12 months by 1996.

instead used it for the wing fixed leading edge "D" spar. Tests on full-scale articles were meanwhile conducted on a rig at Ottobrunn in Germany.

As work began on the structure, engineers were already well advanced with the new interior that had been developed as a mock-up in August 1988. The mock-up included a flight deck, communications center, cockpit-crew rest area, and a fully furnished passenger cabin in a three-class configuration. Foldaway couches were also mocked-up in the doorways to provide rest areas for cabin crew. Recognizing that these were far from ideal, Airbus said the feature would merely supplement a proposed under-floor crew rest area first developed in 1987 in association with Deutsche Airbus. The rest area was based on a 94 inch pallet, shaped like an LD6 cargo container, and installed at the front end of the rear cargo hold. It could be reached by descending a short flight of stairs and generally contained six bunks.

Competing with the slightly wider MD-11 and 777, as Boeing's competing 767-X project had become by 1990, Airbus lavished a lot of attention on various cabin configurations ranging from high-density single-class to long-range three-class layouts. The most complex of all was the A340-300, seating 295 in three classes with 18 first-class "sleeperette" seats at 60 inch pitch, 81 business class seats at 37 inches, and 196 economy seats at 34 inches. In two-class medium range configuration, the aircraft seated 335 with 30 first- and 305 economy class seats. A single-class high-density layout seated 440 in nine-abreast, 31-inch pitch seats.

The shorter A340-200 had optional seating for 262 in three classes with 18 first, 74 business, and 170 economy, or a two-class layout seating 303 with 30 first and 273 in economy. Airbus also proposed an A340-300C Combi with room for 221 passengers and four cargo pallets.

With the imminent rise in production associated with the launch of the A330/A340 and the ramp up in A320 activity, Airbus began urgent negotiations to buy a fifth Super Guppy in September 1988 for delivery in 1992. At this stage, it forecast that A320 production would be at eight per month, while the manufacture of A300s and A310s was expected to stay steady.

In the meantime, the first major tranche of A330/A340 contracts began to be awarded to companies all over the world. Subcontractors were named in Austria, Australia, Canada, China, Greece, Italy, India, Japan, Korea, Portugal, the United States, and the former Yugoslavia. Sundstrand of the United States was selected as the main contractor for the electrical generation system, while Liebherr of West Germany won the contract for the slat transmission actuation system, the flap/slat power control unit wingtip brake, and the air conditioning system.

Lucas in the United Kingdom won deals as a supplier to Liebherr on the first two projects, and Garrett (later to become part of AlliedSignal, then Honeywell) won work with ABG-Semca of France on the air conditioning system. Nord Micro of Germany won a $70 million cabin pressure control system contract while work on the trimming tail actuator was awarded to Bronzavia Airequipment of France.

Dowty Rotol was selected to provide the flap actuation and transmission system in a deal potentially valued at around $200 million. Design and development was carried out with Zahnradfabrik Friedrichshafen (ZF) of Germany. Zahnradfabrik Friedrichshafen was responsible for the rotary drive systems within the flap contract that was less complex than previously expected, largely because Airbus had finally decided to abandon the variable camber wing concept. This was dumped on the basis that the developmental efforts, costs, and risks did not justify the savings.

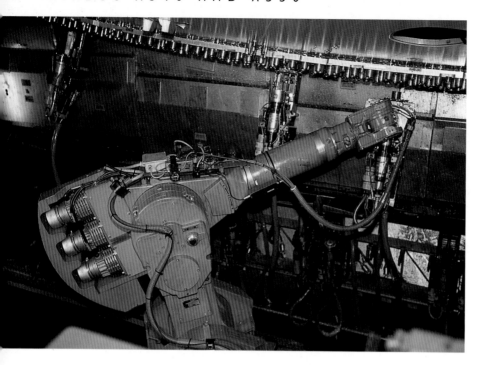

Robots are used to drill mating holes in the wing-to-fuselage assembly process. The system was designed to accommodate eight robots, four to each side, and was estimated by Airbus to save around 20 percent on labor costs and 5 percent on time.

Zahnradfabrik Friedrichshafen also won work to produce the gearbox for the Garrett-developed auxiliary power unit (APU), while fellow German company BGT was awarded the associated electronic control contract, and Turbomeca of France the compressor work. The tail-mounted APU was housed in a self-contained titanium inner skin and aluminum outer-skin compartment in case of a fire, and was developed to drive a 115kVA generator.

Mannesmann-Rexroth joined forces with Hydraulic Research Textron of the United States and Ratier Figeac of France, to become the main contractor for the spoiler/airbrake actuation system in a deal valued at more than $50 million.

Canadair, part of Bombardier, also won a $640 million subcontract to design and build the main landing gear bay lateral panel, the aft pressure bulkhead, and the keel beam in the center section of the aircraft. In the nose section, it was selected to make the lower shell structure, the cockpit center structure, and the nose landing gear doors.

Aerospace Technologies of Australia won floor support structure work, as well as fabrication of the pressure bulkhead separating the cabin from the main landing gear compartment and the central gear hatches. Other suppliers included Yugoslavia's Soko Aircraft Industries that was contracted by Aerospatiale subsidiaries Sogerma and Socea to produce the upper fuselage panels in the central section. Forward upper structures were supplied by Silat in cooperation with Korean Air.

One of the largest single contracts awarded at the time, and valued at $1.2 billion, went to Textron Aerostructures. The U.S. company was responsible for the design and manufacture of the outer leading edge and the four panels of the wing top skin stringer, as well as the outer flap, the flap track fairings, and some spoilers.

Later in October 1988, just as Aerospatiale's Nantes plant started machining the first parts of the A340 wing center section, BAe selected France's Messier-Hispano-Bugatti to design, develop, and manufacture the nose gear. The contract was potentially valued at more than $150 million over the life of the program, and covered the supply of at least 600 units over the next 16 years. The main landing gear contract was meanwhile awarded to Dowty Rotol and its U.S. partner, Cleveland Pneumatic.

By early 1989 the first parts of the prototype A340 were coming together all over the world. The most tangible evidence of progress was at Aerospatiale's Nantes and Saint-Nazaire factories where the wing center sections and fuselage center sections were constructed respectively. The initial work at Saint-Nazaire focused on the assembly of a fuselage center–section mock-up to verify the layout of cables, pipes, and systems. The mock-up was later used with airline customers in reviews of maintenance procedures. In late July 1989, the first A340 wing rib was machined at BAe's Brough site. So far, development had kept perfectly to schedule but sadly this was about to change.

Discontented workers at the recently privatized BAe voted to go on strike in late 1989, just as preparations for the construction of the first A340 wingset were reaching a critical phase. Hoping for a quick settlement, BAe designers meanwhile completed the design of the large winglets that it estimated would cut fuel consumption by about 1.5 percent. The final winglet design was shorter and broader than previously expected, covering approximately 90 percent of the wingtip chord and measuring a little over six feet in length. The winglets were designed to cant out by 42.5 degrees, and were built by Hawker de Havilland in Australia.

At around the same time, final wind tunnel work was underway at the Deutsche-Niederlandischer Windkanal (DNW German Dutch National) facility at Emmeloord in the Netherlands using a one-tenth scale model built by MBB. Weighing more than 3,500 pounds, and with a wingspan in excess of 19 feet, the finely crafted model had geometric toler-

ances of 0.002mm in critical areas of the airframe such as the wing leading edge/fuselage join area.

More contracts for the real thing were still being issued. In October 1989, Airbus awarded major contracts valued at more than $80 million to AlliedSignal and GE for pneumatic systems. The AlliedSignal deal covered main engine starting systems and variable bleed valves for the CFM56, while the GE agreement covered thrust-reverser actuation systems for the A330's CF6-80E1 engine. Westland Aerospace of the United Kingdom, meanwhile, won a $30 million contract to develop a tire pressure indicating system for the new aircraft. Techniphone, part of the French Mors Group, supplied computer hardware and software as well as the pressure cell for the system.

The BAe strike finally ended in March 1990, having lasted 17 long weeks. The impact meant a drop in expected deliveries for the year from 135 aircraft to 104, and a potential two-month slippage in the A330/A340 program. The dispute was calculated to have cost Airbus $250 million and meant that the consortium's long-awaited first annual profit, which had been expected in 1990, was put off for another year. The most immediate impact on the A340 was a much later first flight. This was now put back from the end of September 1991 to some time in October or November.

Following wing-to-fuselage mating, the enormous "backbone" of the aircraft is lifted by traveling crane to the second main assembly section in the Clement Ader building. Here the front and rear fuselage sections are attached in a cycle lasting around 12 hours. The graceful arch and impressive 190 feet span (without winglets) of the completed assembly is seen in this view. Note the large, overhead crane.

Once the fuselage is assembled, the tail, landing gear, and other components are attached and the aircraft is towed to one of four "cells" for finishing and general systems tests. This process was designed to take about nine days after which the aircraft is taken to another hall for engine installation. Note the white painted composite fin and rudder, constructed largely on carbon fiber-reinforced plastic.

By late September 1990, the first wings were finally on their way from Chester to Bremen aboard a lumbering Super Guppy. Each wing section weighed 30,800 pounds and was so large at 107 feet long, that a shipset took two trips to deliver. They were carried on specially developed air transportation trolleys produced by a British tool-making concern called the Hyde Group.

The trolley had to withstand flight loads of +4.5g/-2g vertically, 1.5g sideways, and 6g forwards. To ease road transportation and to squeeze inside the Super Guppy (with just 4 inches to spare!), the wing was canted up on the trolley by 33 degrees using hydraulic rams. The same trolleys were also used to transport the equipped wings, weighing 6,600 pounds more with control surfaces fitted, from Bremen to Toulouse.

The following month, the Clement Ader site was declared formally open for business as workers prepared to begin receiving the first subassemblies in November. Aerospatiale's flight test department meanwhile began setting up a second telemetry ground room at Toulouse and added extra remote satellite down links as it prepared for the start of the flight test effort. Finally, at the end of November, the first sections for A340-300 No.1, a 69-feet long forward fuselage section and a 52-feet long center wing section, arrived by Super Guppy from Saint-Nazaire.

The wings arrived from Bremen by the end of the month, and in January 1991 the rear fuselage, Spanish-built horizontal stabilizer, and Aerospatiale-made engine pylons also arrived "on dock." By the end of the month, the wings were joined to the center fuselage section by a computer-controlled jig, and the first real impressions of the sheer size of the new Airbus began to be felt.

In February 1991 the rear and forward fuselage sections were mated with the center section using the semi-automatic

Cables, conduits, air conditioning ducts, insulation, and the secondary support structure are fitted before cabin linings and furnishings are installed. Composite sandwich panels that form the main cabin floor are supported by machined floor beams.

machined bottom surface of each 90-feet long wing section was made up of four skin panels, the longest of which was almost 70 feet long. Deutsche Airbus was meanwhile completing work on an 18 feet wingspan one-tenth scale model of the A330 for use in the DNW German-Dutch Windtunnel. The model was fitted with two 10-inch diameter turbofan simulators for the tests which were aimed at evaluating the behavior of the big twin in pitch and yaw. The wind tunnel tests finally commenced that October.

By the end of March, the first A340 was substantially complete apart from engines, winglets, a radome, and paint. Workers gathered to see it emerge briefly into daylight as it was towed to have its CFM56-5C2 engines installed. Shortly afterwards, with engines hung on the wing, the aircraft was subjected to intense vibration tests as the buildup to first flight got under way.

Flight tests of the archrival MD-11, which had begun flight tests eight months late on January 10, 1990, were meanwhile revealing some disturbing data that played right into the hands of Airbus. The tests showed fuel burn on the P&W PW4460-powered version was a staggering 6.7 to 8.4 percent above contract specification, while the GE CF6-80C2D1F was between 4.3 and 5.3 percent above the limit. The MD-11 was definitely an underperformer, and fearing an impact on sales, MDC desperately sought to claw back range. It urged the engine makers to make good on their earlier performance promises and embarked on a rigorous performance improvement package (PIP) to reduce drag and weight, as well as increase fuel capacity.

Despite its urgent efforts, airline confidence was badly shaken by the revelations. These reached crisis point when, on August 2, 1991, Singapore Airlines (SIA) canceled its key order for 20 MD-11s. The airline said simply, "The intended purchase of the MD-11 was predicated on the aircraft's ability to perform certain long-haul sectors—Singapore–Paris for example—with defined payload capabilities. While the aircraft is excellent for shorter-range requirements, it has not to date been able to meet SIA's long-haul demands."

The blow was a classic double-whammy for MDC. Not only did it wipe more than $3 billion from its order book, but, worse still, SIA immediately placed orders and options for up to 20 of the competing A340-300s. The $3.35 billion deal for seven firm, seven orders subject to reconfirmation, and six options, was a killer blow from which the MD-11, and ultimately McDonnell Douglas itself, never recovered. Airbus, on

riveting system for the first time. The next month the virtually completed aircraft received its fin, tail plane, undercarriage, and engine pylons.

March also saw the start of manufacturing of the first wing panels for the A330 at BAe's Chester factory. The

Even the people who built these two forward fuselage sections would be unable to differentiate at this stage between one intended for service as an A330 and one to be built as an A340. Forward sections, comprising French-made cockpits and German-made fuselage barrels, are assembled by Airbus France at Aerospatiale's Saint-Nazaire site before being transported to Toulouse.

Engineers complete the complex task of installing and checking out the A340's flight deck. Electronic instrumentation consists of duplicated primary flight displays, navigation displays, and electronic centralized aircraft monitors (ECAM), all controlled by three display management computers. Each of these can control all six displays in four possible formats. Note the absence of the conventional control column and the side-stick, just visible on the far side of the cockpit, with which they have been replaced.

Developed originally by Dowty Aerospace, now Messier-Dowty, the A330/A340 main landing gear was the largest of its type until the subsequent birth of the Boeing 777. The design features an articulating bogie and a shortening mechanism that repositions and closes the oleo shock strut to fit the big gear into the relatively limited stowage area provided on either side of the keel beam. The articulating, or levered gear, allows only the rear wheels to be in contact with the runway at the end of the takeoff run, thereby increasing the effective length of the gear, increasing permissable takeoff angle, and thereby improving performance.

With vital recent sales victories in Europe, the Middle East, and Asia, particularly Singapore, already under its belt, Airbus was in a jubilant mood when it celebrated the rollout of the first A340 at Toulouse on October 4, 1991. Total orders for the combined A330/A340 family at this stage stood at almost 250, and 10 years on was approaching the 700th milestone.

the other hand, could not have been more pleased. Little did it know that just over a year later it would find itself in an uncomfortably similar position.

More good news for Airbus continued to come in with new orders for the A340 from All Nippon Airways and Kuwait Airways, the latter placing a record order for 24 wide-bodies (A310s, A300-600s, and A340s) and five narrow bodies (A320s and A321s). These were intended to replace its fleet that had been almost totally wiped out during the Gulf War following the invasion by Iraq the previous year.

The wave of fresh orders continued and the long-awaited rollout of the A340, on October 4, 1991, coincided with an announcement from Korean Air that it was ordering seven A330s and optioning a further eight. The latest sales flurry meant that total A340 orders stood at 110, while that of the A330 amounted to almost 140. With confidence therefore brimming, Airbus prepared to begin the most ambitious flight test program it had ever attempted.

CHAPTER FIVE

A340 TAKES FLIGHT

With a firm hand, Airbus chief test pilot, Pierre Baud pushed the four throttle levers forward and felt the A340-300 gather pace along the runway. Alongside, engineering test pilot Nick Warner called out speeds as the big jet accelerated towards its predicted takeoff point.

Pictured moments after touchdown at its first port of call outside France, the prototype taxies to the stand at the Singapore airshow in February 1992. The short visit was intended to be a lot more than a publicity stunt, and doubled as a serious test of the aircraft's long-range cruise performance. Given the importance of SIA's order, the visit also carried tremendous diplomatic weight.

It was October 25, 1991, and the moment of truth for Europe's first four-engined, wide-bodied jetliner program. Within seconds, the A340 lifted smoothly off and climbed into the clear sky of southwestern France. With a takeoff weight of around 440,530 pounds, the A340 had more than enough fuel to cross the Atlantic, but instead turned sedately towards the prearranged test area.

Previous Page: Flight testing of the A340 progressed rapidly after its maiden flight on October 25, 1991. By January 1992, the prototype was conducting minimum unstick-speed (Vmu) trials at Toulouse. These tests measured the lowest speed at which the aircraft would takeoff, and involved raising the nose as high as possible to maximize lift with reduced engine power settings. The rear of the fuselage was protected for the tests by a specially mounted skid.

The aircraft was gently coaxed into a climb to higher and higher altitudes, eventually reaching 40,000 feet. The crew also accelerated to the A340's maximum operating speed of 335 knots before pulling back the throttles, dropping the flaps, and easing back the aircraft to perform a slow-speed flight at 120 knots. In a testament to the success of the designers of the FBW flight control system, Baud radioed to the telemetry room that it handled "like the A320." In all, the maiden flight lasted 4 hours 47 minutes, a record for a first flight of any Airbus type.

On landing, the crew seemed very pleased with the performance of the big bird. "If the aircraft had been in airline service, it could have been dispatched on a revenue-earning flight," said Warner, who added, "we wanted to carry out a representative test as soon as possible."

The flight boosted confidence that the planned 14-month, 2,000-hour test program, involving six aircraft, would be essentially trouble-free. Unfortunately for Airbus, this was not to be the case. The consortium was developing the first four-engined wide-bodied jet transport to be certified in the West since the 747, and it was in for a few unpleasant surprises.

Blissfully unaware of the challenges that lay ahead, the first A340 quickly amassed test hours. By early January 1992, it passed the 100-hour benchmark and all seven Airbus pilots who had flown it were unanimous in confirming the similarity of handling characteristics to the A320. Systems reliability continued to be excellent to the extent that Airbus said it could "ensure regular operation in airline service."

By this stage the A340 had already been flown at low speeds down to 100 knots at low altitude, and to Mach 0.85 at 40,000 feet. The aircraft had been flown in various takeoff configurations and at a takeoff weight of 506,600 pounds, or almost 52,000 pounds below the –300's maximum. Handling had also been tested at various center-of-gravity extremes, and the CFM56-5C2 engines were cleared by CFMI for use at the higher 32,500 pound thrust rating.

It was at this stage that envelope clearance began in earnest and with it, the start of flutter trials. Flutter is a poten- tially disastrous condition that can occur when an aerodynamic instability leads to a divergent oscillation of a part of the airframe, usually a control surface. A milder form of this instability manifests itself as a vibration, or buffet. Despite intensive wind tunnel tests and aerodynamic analysis, these phenomenon can remain hidden until flight tests, and this is what happened with the A340.

The buffet condition was discovered as Airbus prepared to introduce the second aircraft to the test program in February, and the third (the first of the longer-range, shorter A340-200s) in March. The problem occurred at low lift coefficients when the airflow around the outer engine pylon would become detached. The result was an unexpectedly severe buffet that worked its way down through the wing to be felt in the cabin. The buffet also meant extra drag, contributing toward poorer than expected fuel consumption performance.

For the moment, Airbus tried to keep news of the problems under wraps. It was a particularly anxious time for the consortium as the aircraft had been dispatched to the Asian Aerospace show in Singapore, home of new customer airline SIA. The aircraft left Toulouse on February 23, 1992, with a takeoff weight of 546,250 pounds. It carried 48,460 pounds of test equipment and burned 176,210 pounds of fuel during the flight to the show—its first appearance outside of France.

Smiles all round as the Airbus test crew, including Airbus managing director Jean Pierson (in jacket), deplanes at Singapore from their 13-hour flight from Toulouse in February 1992. Behind the smiles, however, were serious concerns about the range performance of the new jetliner. Test data, gathered on this very flight, confirmed growing fears among Airbus engineers that the baseline aircraft would not be able to meet the critical Singapore-Paris nonstop mission.

The faintly visible bulge nestled alongside the inboard edge of the engine pylon is the "plastron" aerodynamic modification devised in 1992 as part of efforts to cut drag and improve A340 cruise performance. The modification appears on all subsequent –200 and –300 aircraft along with changes to the inboard slats to increase chord. The bulge is pictured here after being installed on the second A340-300, F-WWAS, at Filton, near Bristol in April 1992.

An unusual view of the second A340-300 prototype as it is towed to the ramp at Filton in April 1992, following modifications to its wings. The picture was taken from the roof of the huge Brabazon building built originally in the 1940s to manufacture the proposed airliner of that name. The same building was later used to assemble the British-built Concorde fleet.

Aware of the emerging performance issues, Airbus declined to give any details of the results of the test program before briefing airline customers who had been invited to a two-day briefing at Toulouse in March. The aircraft left Singapore on February 25, carrying Jean Pierson, and flew directly to Mauritius in the Indian Ocean where it was demonstrated to the national carrier.

Fifteen days later, the Airbus customer group was told that a series of modifications had been devised to bring the A340 back to specification. Although Airbus officially denied persistent—and inevitable—rumors of flutter problems with the outer pylon, it told the airlines about the buffet issue and other flight control changes. One future operator said after the briefing, "We are convinced that the A340 will meet its guaranteed performance by the time it enters service."

The main modification revealed at the conference was an underwing fairing inboard of each outboard engine pylon to solve the flow separation problems. Resembling the breast plate of a knight's suit of armor, the slightly bulged fairing was made of composites, roughly triangular in shape, about 6 inches thick at the pylon and almost 5 feet long on each side. Called the "plastron" by Airbus, it locally redistributed pressure across the chord, thereby improving the aerodynamic flow.

Other changes included a 10 percent chord increase on the outboard portion of the No.1 (inboard) slat, between the root and inboard engine pylon, to relieve a streamwise condition known as "wave" drag. The slat was extended by almost 10 inches at the root end, tapering to no extension at the pylon. At the rootend, this extension was not faired in, but left to form what Airbus called a "saw-tooth."

The activation sequence of the spoilers was also modified to eliminate an overload condition to the center gear experienced by the prototype during landing. Airbus also revealed a change to the spoiler movement in flight, to eliminate buffet from spoilers numbers 2 and 3 in high lift configuration, with flaps down and slats out.

Airbus also planned to inhibit the movement of the outboard ailerons during cruise above 270 knots to relieve a sudden movement, dubbed "aileron jerk," that induced an excessive wing structural response. Henceforward, roll control was to be by spoilers only after ailerons were locked out. Although these aerodynamic improvements were expected to yield a 1 percent reduction in drag, this in fact turned out to be just 0.7 percent.

Longer-term changes envisaged by Airbus for the planned longer-range, heavier-weight versions of the –300 were more dramatic. They included a small increase to the wing incidence

The prototype, F-WWAI, assumed the bulk of the test work in the development and flight certification effort that was wrapped up on December 22, 1992, after a 750-flight, 2,400-hour program involving six aircraft. Retained by Airbus for further development work, it became a regular star performer at airshows. It is pictured taxiing in from yet another display at the 1997 Paris show.

The unexpected 1.5-degree nose-down attitude of the A340, added to its length and raised fears that standard aircraft servicing equipment would not be suitable for use at the rear doors. Airbus studied a nose leg extension to solve the situation, caused by the leg settling short, but early in-service experience proved the modification to be unnecessary.

angle (the angle at which the entire wing is presented to the airstream), through a twist of the airfoil. This was expected to generate between 0.8 and 1 percent range improvement, and was to be accompanied by a change in the thrust vector angle of the outboard engines. Although almost imperceptible, the wing-mounted engines on jet aircraft are "toed" in toward the centerline to produce symmetric thrust. Airbus believed that, by vectoring the thrust down a little, it could get between 0.4 and 0.8 percent improvement. The wing twist change was introduced on later aircraft.

It also looked at putting aerodynamic strakes on the aft fuselage and began a study into the use of a friction-reducing, microgrooved plastic foil developed by 3M called riblets. The foil was applied to the skin like sticky tape and expected to yield significant drag reductions. The study built on test results from a trial conducted by Lufthansa that had carried 12 specimen pieces on an A300-600 in normal scheduled service for a year in 1988, 3M itself, and Airbus. The consortium's continuous quest for technological advantage had also led to an extensive trial of the riblet technology on an A320, of which about 80 percent of the skin was covered for a similar trial in late 1989.

Another change discussed at the meeting was a possible 1-foot 4-inch extension of the nose gear leg to improve ground handling. Early tests revealed concerns that the nose down attitude of the aircraft left the aft service door around 10 inches too high for standard service trucks to reach the sill. An onboard airstair, revised cargo loading system, and raised nose gear design were perfected as a result. Airbus planned to introduce the longer noseleg from line 87 onwards, though the plan was later dropped when in-service experience showed it was not really needed.

Delegates at the conference also took time out to see the almost completed A330 that was later rolled out—still without engines—on March 31, 1992. The following day, the first A340-200 made its maiden flight from a rain-soaked runway at Toulouse and promptly joined the test program that was focused increasingly on improving cruise performance.

Part of this performance recovery also came from engine improvements that were pushed through by CFMI from July 1992. These included the design of an improved combustion chamber and the rerouting of cooling air through the turbine. Flight tests later showed a 1.5 percent fuel burn improvement and further modifications were to add an additional 2 percent by 1995.

The Asian market was a priority for the A330/A340 marketing team from day one, and in October 1992 these efforts began paying off when China Eastern Airlines placed an order for five A340s. The aircraft were to join existing A300-600R, A310-300, and, even more importantly, four McDonnell Douglas MD-11s already in service. In the years leading up to the A340 purchase, the newly autonomous China Eastern saw passenger loads increase rapidly, growing by a staggering 39 percent between 1990 and 1991.

Hot and high tests were completed successfully in Saudi Arabia in July, and in mid-August the second test aircraft was taken on a flight management system validation flight over the North Pole. In the process it also became the first A340 to land in North America, when it was refueled at Fairbanks in Alaska. By this stage six A340s were flying in the certification program that was aimed at completion by the end of the year. More than 1,100 flight hours out of the 2,000 hours planned had also been completed, though Airbus expected the total to go beyond the original predicted target as a result of the many modifications made to the aircraft.

These included software as well as hardware changes. Airbus worked on improvements to the flight management system and automatic landing system, including fine-tuning of the control laws governing the "flare" angle at touchdown. With the center of gravity toward the rear of its range, the flare could last too long, allowing the aircraft to use up excessive runway before touching down.

Further work remained on softening the reaction of the FBW flight control system to turbulence, both in longitudinal and lateral axes. The control laws were also modified to remove the possibility that a pilot's continual adjustments on the side-stick during a gusty final approach could get in phase with the fuselage's 3Hz natural longitudinal flexing frequency. Although not a problem technically, test pilot Nick Warner remarked, "We didn't want passengers remarking that the

A340 always gave a bouncy landing." Airbus also spent time working on explanations and fixes for a persistent two degrees nose-up attitude in the cruise, and worked on sound-proofing solutions for the forward cabin.

While tests pushed on, Airbus sales teams focused on campaigns around the world. The wide-body market was globally depressed in the aftermath of the Gulf War and the subsequent worldwide economic impact, but China appeared largely immune from these effects. Sure enough in October, China Eastern Airlines ordered five A340s, marking the first confirmed sale of the A330/A340 family to China.

Later the same month, Airbus revealed design changes to the rudder control after flight tests showed it was producing greater side-force than desired. Describing the change as a "tweak," Airbus altered the rudder to reduce the amount of travel needed to reach full deflection. At around the same time, it also began investigative work on drag-reducing "pylon cuffs" or fillet fairings, as well as nacelle-mounted aerodynamic strakes for the outboard engines. This latter feature improved low-speed handling.

Meanwhile fatigue tests got underway at German airframe fatigue-test specialists IABG at Ottobrunn. The test site carried out 40,000 simulated flights on the A340, before eventually being reconfigured to do the same tests on the A330. The company changed the original plan to use a life factor of three for the tests, after deciding the resulting six-year long test period was too long. The A340's life was taken as 20,000 landings and takeoffs, while the A330's life was considered to be double this number. Instead a decision was made to increase the load factor from the standard 1g to 1.1g and reduce the life factor to two—a procedure first used for the Fokker 100.

The tests included a maximum wing deformation of up to 10 feet above normal position, and close to 4 feet below. The maximum upward deformation was considered equal to a maximum gust load of 3,000 feet per minute. The structure in the fatigue test rig did not incorporate the strengthened wing spar, introduced on the A330 as a result of a static test failure the previous year (see chapter 6). The German company said that "recalculations of the safety factor were carried out, showing the allowables were high enough."

By now all eyes were on SIA and its—as yet—unconfirmed critical order for 20 aircraft. Airbus had designated the special high gross-weight variant for SIA the A340-300X, and was desperate to keep SIA on the order book. The long-range mission requirement that had killed the MD-11 order now threatened to do the same thing to the A340, unless Airbus could convince the airline it had clawed enough performance back.

The SIA aircraft was expected to have a maximum take-off weight of 588,100 pounds, which included a fourth 350-liter water tank that the airline insisted on to ensure an adequate supply to the cabin on ultra-long haul flights. In the following two years, the higher gross weight aircraft was renamed the –300E, and its weight climbed up to 597,500 pounds with an option to 606,300 pounds.

The performance shortfall of the first aircraft had been around 5 percent off its internally set target. The subsequent airframe and engine improvements had reduced this to 4 percent and the remaining improvements were expected to improve the range by a further 2 percent by 1995. SIA had originally signed for delivery of its first aircraft in the latter part of this year, but the extent of the modifications and structural changes meant a six-month slippage to April 1996. Changes included strengthened landing gear and attach-

Lufthansa replaced DC-10-30s with its first A340-200s on the Frankfurt–New York services early in 1992 and discovered it used around 30 percent less fuel as similar loads. For the first time on a wide-body, the airline limited seats to just six abreast in business class. It also spent $5 million on a new suite of cabin comforts, including new 12-channel personal video systems for first-class and business class passengers, and an eight-channel digital compact disc sound system for economy class.

ments, a beefed-up main wing box, and reinforcement of the pickup structure for the nose and main undercarriage legs.

It was not all gloomy tidings, however. Tests had revealed that under some conditions the baseline aircraft was more than 8,000 pounds lighter than predicted and when it was completely empty weighed around 1,100 pounds less than expected. In addition, fuel volume was 1,660 U.S. gallons greater than the original specification.

December brought a mixture of good and bad news for the program. The best news was the award of dual certification on December 22 of both the A340-200 and –300 by the 18 European Joint Aviation Authorities (JAA). The milestone came after the completion of a 750-flight, 2,400-hour flight test effort and also marked the first time the JAA had certified two variants of a brand new airliner simultaneously. The U.S. FAA followed up with certification on May 27, 1993.

The other good news for Airbus was confirmation of the SIA order for 7 firm and 13 optioned A340-300Es. The two events, coupled with the feeling of relief felt by the consortium after months of growing uncertainty over the SIA deal, came

as a welcome boost after a bout of order cancellations. The most devastating of these had been Northwest's cancellation of orders and options for 50 A320s and 24 A340s. Undeterred, Airbus went back to the negotiating table to attempt to reverse Northwest's decision. They were ultimately successful; Northwest later reordered A320s and, finally, in 2001, a batch of A330s.

Into Service

Airbus handed over the first 228-passenger A340-200 to Lufthansa in Frankfurt on February 2, 1993. The German airline announced plans to use the A340 to replace DC-10s on its Frankfurt-New York services (both Newark and JFK), as well as put the new quad jet on routes to Boston, Atlanta, Washington D.C., Dallas-Fort Worth, and Houston. Flight training of 37 pilots and check captains began later the same month at Sharjah, Saudi Arabia, in the run-up to service entry scheduled for March 15.

Air France took its first A340-300 on February 26, and planned to operate nine of the total of 19 A340s on order by

Air France introduced its first A340-300s into revenue service in late March 1992, replacing Boeing 747s on the Paris-Washington route. It followed with twice-weekly A340 Paris-Mexico services, along with five-times weekly Paris-Houston-Mexico flights. By August that year Paris was linked by A340 with Buenos Aires, Argentina. Services to Santiago, Chile and Recife and Sao Paulo, Brazil, followed by the end of 1992.

A Singapore Airlines A340-300E touches down at Beijing after the relatively short flight from its island base. The first high gross-weight derivative, aircraft number 117, flew in August 1995 and SIA took delivery of its first aircraft (number 123) in April 1996. The aircraft later became a pawn in the on-going Airbus-Boeing war when the U.S. manufacturer agreed to buy the A340s from the airline for eventual onward sale, as part of a deal to buy 777s.

the end of 1993. Of these, seven had been ordered directly by UTA, which it now owned, and five were to be leased from Sabena, the Belgian airline in which Air France had a 35 percent stake. Air France used its A340s to replace 747s on the Paris-Washington D.C. run four times a week. This gradually moved to a daily operation as more A340s joined the fleet. Other A340 routes included Paris to Houston and Mexico City, as well as Paris to Buenos Aires, Santiago, Recife, Sao Paulo, Montreal, and Miami.

By a strange, though not altogether unexpected twist, the first Air France A340 also happened to be the 1,000th Airbus aircraft to leave the consortium's Toulouse facility since the initial A300 delivery in May 1974, again to Air France. Underlining the growing success of Airbus, it was interesting to note that the 500th delivery had occurred only four years before the A340 milestone handover.

Throughout the latter stages of the certification program, both Air France and Lufthansa conducted extensive route-proving flights as part of the most extensive flight test effort ever undertaken by Airbus. The Lufthansa aircraft undertook

40 flights, lasting a total of 141 hours 25 minutes. Almost 54,000 nautical miles were flown, the longest leg being a non-stop Frankfurt-Honolulu flight covering 6,650 nautical miles in 15 hours 20 minutes. Air France conducted 29 flights for a total of 140 hours 45 minutes, its longest leg being Singapore-Paris (6,220 nautical miles), covered in 14 hours 30 minutes. During flight tests, an A340-200 with a 59,470-pound payload completed a record flight from Toulouse to Perth, Australia, flying the route in 16 hours 22 minutes and arriving with almost four hours of fuel left.

The flights unearthed a few problems mainly with the air conditioning system. However, there were no mechanical failures to systems, airframes, or engines, and no major avionics systems needed changing. The tests had the added benefit of proving that the nose-down issue was not, in fact, an issue at all and did not interfere with ground handling operations.

In general, Lufthansa was "extremely pleased" with the performance of the A340, and reported that low-speed performance was "much better" than predicted. As a result, it felt maximum takeoff weight could be increased by up to 7,700

Testing at Toulouse maintained a furious pace throughout the 1990s as new derivatives of the A320 family joined the growing throng of A330s and A340s coming off the line. Note the prototype A330 in the background by the Clement Ader assembly building, as a test A340 takes to the air on a cross-crew qualification development flight in 1994.

pounds (to 566,080 pounds) for the same thrust. The new engine strakes also reduced A340-300 approach speeds by about 8 knots.

Lufthansa expected to introduce all 15 A340s on firm order by the end of 1994, and planned to replace 747-200 Combis used on some routes. After initial services began to New York, daily flights began to Boston and Atlanta in September and to Washington D.C. and Sao Paulo in October.

With the focus very definitely still on proving the long-range capabilities of the A340, even with reduced payloads, Airbus decided to stage a one-stop, around-the-world flight as a publicity stunt during the 1993 Paris air show. The first A340-200 prototype, suitably named World Ranger for the special flight, left Le Bourget in Paris at 11:58 local time on June 16 and landed back there at 12:20 local time two days later, having flown around the globe via New Zealand.

The flight took only 22 minutes and 6 seconds longer than two days and, barring the enthusiastic reception which greeted them in Auckland, would probably have been achieved in even less time. Six world records were broken during the flight, including the longest nonstop flight by any airliner—the 10,409 nautical miles from Auckland to Paris and the fastest around-the-world in its class.

Unlike a previous range record flight in 1989 in which a Qantas-operated 747-400 had flown direct from Heathrow to Sydney, Australia, with 18 people on board, the A340 had

Cathay Pacific Airways, along with Lufthansa, agreed with Airbus in late 1996 to cover the upper fuselage, vertical tail, and tailplane of their A340s with a thin-film, microscopic, drag-reducing skin developed by 3M. The skin was designed to cut fuel burn by 1 percent by cutting boundary layer or surface turbulence. Although trials proved some benefits, maintenance issues revealed that the technology was still immature at the time. Hong Kong-based Cathay initially leased a batch of A340s originally destined for Philippine Airlines, before buying a fleet of high gross-weight versions.

Pilots took readily to the side-stick controls and the A330/A340 fly-by-wire flight control system. This is programmed to protect the aircraft from being overstressed and automatically limits bank angle to 33 degrees in normal flight, and to 67 degrees with the stick held full-over to one side. If the stick is held fully forward, the system automatically raises the nose of the aircraft when airspeed reaches Vmo (maximum operating velocity) plus 15 knots (17 mph). If the stick is held fully back, and speed allowed to decay, the throttles automatically move forward to full power.

standard fuel and was not towed to the threshold of the runway for engine start-up. The 747 record delivery flight had been achieved using special high-density (0.84 specific gravity) fuel and the aircraft had been towed to the end of the runway before starting up. It used 395,374 pounds of fuel and landed with only 8,810 pounds remaining!

The A340's only nonstandard equipment for the mission was five additional center tanks (ACTs) in the rear cargo hold, carrying a total of 62,775 pounds of fuel. The ACTs were optional for the A330 and A340, but by this stage Airbus believed the standard range of the A340 had proved itself more than adequate for every anticipated route.

The world record attempt was different, however. Instead of the standard seating for 263, the aircraft had no cabin trim, temporary galley and toilet arrangements, 450 pounds of spares, and 32 seats for 22 people on board. Two crews shared the journey led by Pierre Baud, who by now had been named vice president for the flight division. Others included Airbus test and development director Gerard Guyot, senior vice president of engineering Bernard Ziegler, and engineering test pilot Nick Warner. Flight test engineer Jean Marie Mathios kept a watchful eye on the aircraft and its systems, but was not called into action.

Pilots took turns to sleep on air beds in the cabin, and grabbed up to five hours sleep on each leg. The outbound run to New Zealand took 21 hours 32 minutes and consumed 27,620 pounds of fuel, leaving 31,940 pounds in the tanks. The return leg, after a five-hour stop in Auckland (90 minutes longer than planned), took 21 hours 46 minutes and consumed 29,690 pounds of fuel, leaving 14,300 pounds unused.

Airbus continued to focus on solving in-service issues and teething problems, finding new customers, evolving the design, working on derivatives, and supporting the growing fleet. One of its initial technology items was the successful certification, in late 1993, of a Litton-made global positioning system (GPS). Although it was still too early to use GPS as the sole means of navigation, both the airlines and Airbus knew it was coming and the Litton certification, followed shortly after by a Honeywell GPS approval, provided a good foundation.

The end of 1993 saw yet another boost for the A340 when Cathay Pacific Airways, a predominantly Boeing 747 and Lockheed L-1011 user, agreed to lease six A340s as a prelude to buying up to 12 A340-300Es. The leased aircraft were originally intended for Philippine Airlines (PAL), but had become the center of an embarrassing dispute between Airbus and the airline over nondelivery. Philippine Airlines originally ordered the A340s as part of a fleet renewal plan that included four 747-400s. But the deal was opposed by a PAL shareholder, tobacco tycoon Lucio Tan (who later ousted chairman Antonio Cojuangco). Philippine Airlines then announced it could not

Spot the difference. Apart from the tell-tale throttle quadrant and a few engine displays on the screens, this could be either an A330 or an A340. Airbus planned the cross-crew qualification benefit to extend beyond the big new jetliners to include the cockpits of the extremely similar A320 family. Crews from the A320 are able to train for the much larger A340 in as few as 10 days, plus four more days line training, compared to two or three months on other types.

afford to introduce the A340s and 747s and tried to defer the former. Airbus insisted PAL honor its $560 million contract, but agreed to lease the aircraft to Cathay Pacific Airways on condition that it place firm orders for the A340-300X (-300E).

By August 1994, Airbus and PAL had resolved their differences—with the airline taking four of the aircraft on a six-year lease starting in 1996. In return, Airbus agreed to cancel the carrier's remaining two A340 orders. Cathay, meanwhile, agreed to lease the original four A340-200s on an interim two-year deal.

While it struggled with awkward customers, Airbus also worked hard to satisfy its existing ones. Despite a trouble-free start, the type's operational reliability—the measure of services dispatched on time and completed as planned—averaged only 95.6 percent over the 12 months from May 1993 to May 1994, and fell to 94 percent at the end of January 1994.

Although new aircraft are prone to problems, Airbus believed this performance was unacceptable and worked on improvements to three key problem areas. The first was an inner fuel tank that, before the aircraft entered service, the FAA ruled should be split into two.

Airbus quickly reworked the whole area and fitted new fuel probes, wiring, and computers that consequently had entered service before being fully "shaken down." The revised

system worked well, however, and by mid-1994 the reliability rates had already begun to climb back toward 98 percent. The changes were incorporated into newly built aircraft and were also retrofitted into the fleet by mid-1995.

The second problem area involved the vacuum-type lavatory that required modifying. A third issue was the air conditioning system that exhibited problems with ducting and temperature control.

A key victory in August 1994, and one that was vital to Airbus's long-term family-based marketing drive, was FAA certification of its cross-crew qualification (CCQ) program. This allowed pilots to hold common type-ratings on all Airbus types from the A320 to the A340 and offered huge savings in training costs to airlines operating multiple Airbus types. Under CCQ, an A320 pilot could convert to the A340 with 13 days "differences" training. This was roughly half the time normally required. The CCQ was made feasible by the high degree of commonality between the flight decks of the A320 and A330/A340 families as well as the use of FBW flight control systems.

Federal Aviation Administration approval for CCQ effectively put the stamp of approval on Airbus' family strategy and, just as importantly, the place of the A340 within that family. The A340, it seemed, had well and truly arrived.

CHAPTER SIX

A330 TAKES FLIGHT

W ith the limelight on the A340, the development and construction of the first A330 twin proceeded, by comparison, in an almost stealth-like atmosphere. Final assembly of the first A330, the tenth aircraft on the combined A330/A340 assembly line, began with the wing-fuselage joining process in mid-February 1992. Six weeks later, on March 31, the long "green" fuselage (still in its protective anticorrosion undercoat) was rolled out into the sun for the first time.

The lack of engines exaggerates the slender look of the wings on this A330 as the first aircraft, pictured here at Toulouse on March 31, 1992, was rolled out of the general assembly work station for the first time. The aircraft was fitted with General Electric CF6-80E1 engines the following month and began ground vibration trials in June, prior to first flight.

The big GE CF6-80E1 engines were installed and, by August, the aircraft was basically complete and undergoing vibration tests. Fueling and pressurization tests were on schedule and everything looked good for a trouble-free run-up to the first flight that was scheduled for the end of October.

It was then that trouble struck the program at the worst possible time—right in the middle of the Farnborough air show. First came the news that Northwest Airlines, one of the biggest and most important customers for the big twin, had deferred acceptance of the 16 A330s it had ordered for delivery between 1994 and 1996. Then came the potentially terminal news that the A330 wing had suffered a failure in static tests.

Previous Page: The A300-600 like inboard wing trailing edge, flap track fairing arrangement, and hybrid winglet shape dates this early A330 artists impression to mid-1987. The A330 would take advantage of the wing modifications then being designed for the A340 to help make up for the loss of the SuperFan engine choice on that variant earlier that year.

Remarkably, Airbus had managed to keep news of the failure quiet since it occurred on the static test rig the previous April. On the back of the success of the structural tests it had even announced, two months after the incident, the availability of a higher gross-weight A330-300 version with a 39,650-pound heavier takeoff weight.

While it was unfortunate for Airbus to have the story revealed at a major international show, the delay had enabled it to work out a fix. Just as importantly, BAe designers and engineers had since discovered that the weakness was peculiar to the A330, despite it being a common wing to both models.

The failure had occurred in the rear spar "slightly below" the 1.5 design load target strength and resulted in some deformation. Analysis showed the problem was not as serious as first thought. "It needs only a little bit of local reinforcement. This could occur either in the production phase or perhaps as a retrofit," said Airbus, adding that the problem would not delay the first flight.

A month after the wing failure revelations, on October 14, 1992, Airbus rolled out the first A330 at Toulouse. Deter-

Trouble hit the A330-300 program even before the first aircraft was completed when the static test airframe suffered an unexpected failure in the rear spar early in 1992. Structural reinforcements were designed and added to subsequent aircraft, an example of which is seen here on the line in 1998 prior to delivery to Korean Air.

mined not to let the overcast, drizzly conditions dampen their enthusiasm, Airbus planned to build on the lessons learned from the A340 and run a quick-fire test program that would involve six aircraft and cover around 1,800 hours.

The test effort got off to a good start with a record 5 hour 15 minute maiden flight on November 2. The world's biggest ever twin-engined airliner took off at a weight of 400,880 pounds, some 46,250 pounds of which was made up of test equipment. The aircraft was flown through a large number of test points, covering a wide variety of speeds, heights, and configurations with landing gear raised and lowered.

During the flight, the crew took the big twin close to the edge of stalling, then accelerated all the way up to 330 knots maximum operating speed, and Mach 0.83. The sortie also included high-altitude flight up to a maximum height of 41,000 feet.

By February 1993, it was clear to Airbus that it had a potential winner on its hands. Flight-testing progressed flawlessly and even Pierre Baud said the program was "absolutely

without problems." Testing over the first 160 hours had gone so well, in fact, that Airbus slashed the planned test program down to 985 hours – or almost 1,000 hours less than the original plan. Baud attributed much of the success of the A330 test effort to experience gained during the flight testing of the A340, which he admitted was "very difficult" for the first few months.

Significant "lessons learned" included development of the flight control laws that took just 20 hours on the A330, against the eight months taken for the A340. This was largely because the A340's wings were more flexible than predicted which led to concerns about divergent oscillation (flutter). As a result, it took longer than expected to adjust the FBW flight control system, and allow the full performance envelope to be explored.

"But that work was totally relevant to the A330," said Baud. "If we put aside the fact that a twin performs better than a four," the flying behavior of the two aircraft is such that "I could walk blindfolded into the cockpit of the A330 and not know the difference from an A340." Indeed, the only physical

General Electric CF6-80E1s powered the maiden flight of the A330-300 on November 2, 1992. The prototype, then designated a –301, was later reengined with Rolls-Royce Trent 772s and converted to a –342. In January 1994 it became the first Airbus to fly with Rolls-Royce engines. This unique and well-tested aircraft went on to be delivered to Cathay Pacific Airways in October 1996. *Airbus*

differences of note were the addition of two additional engine throttle levers, and related engine displays on the A340.

While tests went well, marketing did not. The A330 had entered a serious sales drought, and not a single new A330-300 order had been taken since December 1990 when Korean Air ordered seven. Although this same order was reconfirmed in October 1991, new sales were to remain elusive until July 1995, when Aer Lingus signed for the aircraft. Worse still, the booked orders continued to be eroded by cancellations. Northwest's earlier withdrawal was followed, in March 1993, by that of Continental Airlines. The financially troubled U.S. carrier canned firm orders worth $4.2 billion for 20 A330/A340s together with 18 options. Boeing, on the other hand, continued to take orders for its new twin-engined 777.

It was against this increasingly bleak background that Airbus decided it urgently needed to expand the operational flexibility of its new big twin. This meant obtaining early clearance for it to fly on extended-range twin-engine operations (ETOPS) routes as soon as possible. The Boeing 767 and Airbus A310 had pioneered the development of ETOPS routes, primarily across the North Atlantic, throughout the late

Stable mates pictured together during a lull in the A330's busy flight test development and certification effort. Despite the choice of three engine types, basic type certification of all versions of the A330-300 was completed by November 1994—two years after first flight, and a year after this image was captured at the 1993 Dubai air show.

With flight tests going well, and a second aircraft on the verge of entering the program, Airbus showcased the prototype A330-300 at the 1993 Paris air show. By now the sales team needed all the help it could get. Orders had dried up completely, and as part of efforts to rejuvenate sales, Airbus early that year decided to react to Boeing's ETOPS out of the box initiative for the 777 by seeking accelerated ETOPS clearance for the A330. The move marked a fundamental shift in strategy for the A330/A340 concept, and ultimately reaped major rewards for Airbus as a result.

1980s. The fundamental idea was that the new twin-engined jetliners were so reliable that they could operate on routes that took them more than one hour single-engined flying time away from a diversionary airfield.

Gradually, as experience showed statistically fewer diversions and potential causes for problems, ETOPS clearance was extended to 90 minutes, and then to 120 minutes and ultimately to 180 minutes. Airbus knew that Boeing was planning to introduce its A340 rival, the 777, into service already cleared for 180 minutes ETOPS. This meant that no time would be used up actually proving the validity of the aircraft's engines and systems reliability in service. Everything would have to be proven up front to the airworthiness authorities, before entry into service.

Airbus outlined a plan for a more gradual "accelerated" ETOPS approval, a step back from the "ETOPS out of the box" plan hatched by Boeing. The A330 plan, if accepted, would eventually enable operators to fly on one engine up to three hours from a suitable airport in 1995 the same year that the 777 would enter service. The plan called for the A330 to enter service with each of the three engine types with a 90-minute ETOPS approval, to be followed by 120 minutes after 25,000 cumulative engine hours, and 180 minutes after 50,000 engine hours. This compared with traditional requirements calling for between 100,000 and 250,000 engine hours on the first ETOPS-cleared aircraft.

The plan included clearing the GE-powered A330 to 90 minutes by December 1993, and 180 minutes by July 1995.

Thai Airways International became the first Asian-based A330 operator when it inaugurated services with its initial PW4000-powered aircraft on December 19, 1994. Right behind it, literally, came Cathay Pacific Airways, which received its first Rolls-Royce Trent 700-powered A330-300 on February 27, the following year. Here the respective versions, in appropriate order, head for the active runway at Hong Kong's now closed Kai Tak International Airport.

The A330's engines are mounted at the same location as the inboard engines of the A340. The powerplants are attached to the front spar with a huge machined titanium forging, fail-safe attachment links, and a single spigot fitting. The rear pylon attachments are made up of dual triangular and single-link fittings.

The P&W-powered version would get 90-minute clearance in July 1994 and 180-minute in February 1995, while the R-R version would obtain 90-minute clearance in April 1995 and 180-minute ETOPS a year later.

To back up the plan, Airbus also enrolled the A340 and the experience that operators such as Lufthansa and Air France had gained with it, as a way of validating ETOPS-related maintenance. In addition, Airbus planned to run a dedicated 25-hour flight test effort to evaluate the A330 and its systems in failure conditions over the Atlantic. The consortium was confident of its plan, not least because it described the A330 as a "second-generation ETOPS aircraft." Even on standby

Delivery of PW4000-powered A330 aircraft, like these bound for Malaysia Airlines and Thai Airways International, was held up several months in late 1994 by problems with the engine thrust reverser. Deliveries of A340s, such as the aircraft in the foreground, were meanwhile accelerating. This particular A340-300 was delivered to TAP Air Portugal in December that year.

power, for example, the A330 would still have lots of systems that on earlier aircraft would not have been available with only a single engine left working. These included critical bad weather operation systems such as windshield anti-ice, landing lights, weather radar, and precision approach capability. The bigger engines also meant crews would be able to maintain a higher engine-out altitude, and fly above bad weather below.

In August 1993, Airbus conducted a series of live ETOPS demonstrations over the Atlantic in which airline, FAA, and

JAA pilots dealt with unplanned worse-case scenario emergencies. The first flight, from Toulouse to Gander, diverted to Santa Maria in the Azores with a simulated engine failure. The next was a departure from Santa Maria to Montreal, with a simulated generator failure. During the flight, a failure of the other generator and its associated engine, plus APU failure, were simulated. This "absolute worst-case ETOPS scenario" resulted in power being available only from a single hydraulically driven generator.

The third flight was from Gander to Toulouse, with a turn back to Gander after a simulated emergency. The aircraft returned to 22,000 feet where the APU could maintain normal cabin pressurization. Finally, on a Gander to Toulouse flight, it diverted to Shannon, Ireland, after a simulated engine and pressurization failure requiring a 180-minute diversion at 10,000 feet and 300 knots.

Malaysia Airlines (MAS), meanwhile, announced its plans to be the first A330 ETOPS operator from 1994

Turning hard to starboard on final approach to Hong Kong's Kai Tak International by the once-famous checkerboard, a brand new MAS A330-300 sweeps in from Kuala Lumpur. The red and white painted wall was a visual marker to crews negotiating the curved approach path and is now a peeling, forgotten backdrop of Kowloon city.

onwards when it expected to accept the first of up to 10 P&W-powered aircraft to join the fleet. The aircraft were to be used on at least two ETOPS routes, from Kuala Lumpur, Malaysia, to Perth, Australia, and Madras, India. Both routes required a 90-minute ETOPS clearance, while a third route under consideration, Kuala Lumpur to Johannesburg, South Africa, required 120 minutes for more economical operation.

The South African service, previously flown using DC-10-30s, would be nonstop westbound with a technical stop in Mauritius on the return. At 90-minute diversion time, this route had to be flown north of the Great Circle route from Kuala Lumpur to Mauritius, adding another 90 nautical miles to the optimum track. The remaining sector from the Indian

Ocean island to South Africa could be flown direct, thanks to an alternative airfield at Antananarivo on Madagascar.

Malaysia Airlines subsequently became the first operator to be involved in the A330 route proving trials, which began in Kuala Lumpur on August 26, 1993. The trials involved flights on 31 representative sectors totaling 120 flight hours, and included legs from the capital to Penang, Jahore Bahru, Jakarta, Seoul, Taipei, and Tokyo. The aircraft also made one long-haul trip to Johannesburg on August 31 under ETOPS conditions.

The aircraft flown on the trials was the 30th off the A330/A340 line and the first of the large twins to be fitted with a full commercial interior. The MAS trials were followed in September by four days of trials with French airline Air Inter. Unlike the Malaysian tests, the Air Inter A330 carried a full passenger load, mainly airline staff, with turnaround times limited to 45 minutes.

Although MAS had ordered the P&W-powered A330, all the trials were conducted with a GE-powered aircraft and it was not until October 14, 1993, that the P&W PW4168-powered version made its first flight. Certification tests of the GE aircraft were by then nearly completed after almost 1,100 hours flown, and the first flight of the Rolls-Royce-powered variant was coming up quickly with a target date in January 1994.

Finally, on October 21, the A330 became the first aircraft in the world to gain joint U.S. and European certification. The ceremony at Toulouse marked the end of a 1,114-hour, 426-flight test program with the GE engine costing $70 million.

Certification coincided with the results of weight trials that revealed the A330 was 1,100 pounds lighter than expected. For Airbus and the new A330 operators this welcomed news translated into an operational 6,600 pound increase in maximum payload. Cargo capacity effectively increased to 37,440 pounds on ranges of less than 3,000-nautical miles.

Air Inter, or Air France Europe as it was then known, was the first to take advantage of this when it accepted the initial A330 on December 30, 1993. Just over two weeks later, on January 17, 1994, the A330 finally entered commercial service

when it operated a series of flights between Orly airport in Paris, and Marseille.

Development work on the alternate powered variants was meanwhile progressing, with the P&W PW4168 version the first to follow the GE-powered A330 into the air on October 14, 1993. Aircraft serial number 42 was flown from Toulouse for 3 hours 28 minutes on a maiden flight covering low- and high-speed performance up to a ceiling of 41,000 feet. Rated at 68,000 pounds of thrust each, the PW4000 engines were the most powerful engines ever fitted on a civil airliner at the time.

The prototype A330 had, in the interim, had its GE-engines removed and a pair of Rolls-Royce Trent 700s installed in their place. On January 31, 1994, two weeks after the first GE-powered version entered service, it became the first Airbus to fly with the British manufacturer's engines. Together with the BAe-built wings, the presence of R-R engines gave this particular A330 more than 50 percent British content by dollar value. The initial flight lasted 4 hours 45 minutes and reached a maximum speed of Mach 0.86, and an altitude of 41,000 feet. As the Trent was a completely new engine to

A Pratt & Whitney-powered Korean Air A330-300 trundles along a taxiway at Beijing, China, before taking off for Seoul. Pratt & Whitney developed the 64,000 pound thrust PW4164 for the A330-321 model and the higher powered 60,000-pound thrust PW4168 for the –322 version.

The iridescent tail feathers of this Garuda A330-300 underline the tropical origin of this flight, inbound from its base at Jakarta, Indonesia. Note the Rolls-Royce Trent engines, clearly distinguished by their long-duct nacelles.

Airbus, the test program was more extensive and involved two aircraft over a planned 600-hour flight test effort.

The P&W program progressed relatively smoothly toward the planned certification target of June until problems began emerging with the engine's composite thrust reverser. During post-flight inspections, engineers discovered that sections of the multilayered composite skins were delaminating under the pressure of continued use. Reversers were a very sensitive issue at the time with P&W, problems with another reverser mechanism having been at the heart of a recent crash of a Lauda Air Boeing 767-300ER in Thailand.

The problems centered on a loss of bonding in several areas of the composite inner-cowling, manufactured by Martin Marietta, and did not affect any moving parts of the cascade-type reverser that had been certified by the FAA that May. Although the PW4168 reverser had the highest propor-

tion of composites of any system built by Martin Marietta at the time, the U.S. company felt confident it could solve the problems. Inevitably with such a concentrated test effort, the problems caused delays, and launch customers MAS and Thai Airways International were told to expect a three-month slip in deliveries.

While P&W and Martin Marietta worked around the clock to correct the problems, Airbus pressed on with supplementary certification test flights. It was on one such flight, on June 30, 1994, that disaster struck.

A P&W-powered A330-300, aircraft number 42, was being used to test a new autopilot standard for PW4000-powered versions for bad weather (category three) operations. The plan was to test the ability of the control laws in the autopilot to safely fly the aircraft during a worst-case scenario. This was maximum aft center of gravity (42 percent), minimum go-around speed, high rate of climb, and engine failure.

The aircraft was captained by Airbus chief test pilot Nick Warner, and flown by Michel Cais, an Air Inter training captain working for the Airbus training organization, Aeroformation. Also aboard were five others, including Airbus test

Production of the A330-300 gradually increased throughout the 1990s from just two in 1992 to 37 in 1997, after which numbers hovered in the 30s for subsequent years. The Clement Ader site was geared to handle a maximum build rate of around 14 A330/A340s per month, though average output was just over five per month with a total of 62 produced in 2000. Production rates are slated to increase to eight per month by 2003.

engineers, and a visiting captain from KLM. The takeoff was the second in a sortie designed to test the new autopilot system. During the first takeoff, the crew had flown engine-out go-arounds twice. They then made a full-stop landing and taxied around for another takeoff.

The sortie by this time had already lasted 55 minutes, and the tired crew failed to reset the altitude-capture on the altitude from 2,000 feet to a more normal height of around 7,000 feet. The setting meant that the aircraft's FBW system was geared within seconds of takeoff to try to maintain altitude, rather than protecting the attitude (or flying angle) of the aircraft to ensure that it would not stall. The cancellation of the attitude-limiting function was a perfectly acceptable situation while the autopilot was switching between modes. In normal circumstances this would never have posed a danger, but the unusual conditions of the test, added to several other factors, was to prove fatal.

Unaware of their error, the crew set maximum thrust on the engines, accelerated rapidly down the runway for 25 seconds to 135 knots and soared quickly into a steep climb. To maintain climb speed of 150 knots, Cais pulled the aircraft into a 25-degree climb angle – almost 11 degrees higher than

the previous takeoff. After six seconds, climbing now at 150 knots, the autopilot was engaged and the number one (left) engine was pulled back to idle, simulating a failure. At the same time, one of the hydraulic systems was disabled, to add another degree of difficulty to the simulation.

As expected, the aircraft's pitch angle started to decrease, but not as far as required. Warner had been expecting the autopilot to engage and reduce the A330's steep nose-high attitude to a more controllable 18 degrees. Warner frantically tried three times to engage the mode and, in the meantime, became unaware of the rapid decay in airspeed.

As the A330 slowed through 100 knots, the aircraft's built-in angle-of-attack protection system (alpha protect) activated as the alpha passed 14 degrees. Another system called alpha-floor then activated, and automatically began to spool up the throttled-back left engine.

Rapidly realizing how critical the situation was, Warner believed the best chance of escape was to take manual control. He overrode the alpha-floor system by throttling back on the right engine, and pushed the sidestick fully forward. Unfortunately his actions came approximately 1.5 seconds too late, and the aircraft was already doomed. The aircraft was very low,

Cathay Pacific Airways became a firm fan of the A330, ordering 20 of the type, despite also operating Boeing 777-200s and the A340. As with neighboring Hong Kong carrier Dragonair, Cathay used the new twin principally to replace aging Lockheed L-1011 TriStars on regional Asian routes to Japan, Korea, China, Indonesia, and Singapore.

Philippine Airlines was one of the earliest Pacific rim operators of the A330 and A340. Having ordered eight examples of each, the financially troubled carrier ended up flying all eight A330s and four A340s. Note the prominent 9-foot tall winglets, which can be detached in the event of damage.

at around 1,300 feet, and airspeed had dropped to 90 knots, well below the minimum control speed of 118 knots required with maximum asymmetric power.

The A330 suddenly banked 110 degrees to the left and although Warner remarkably managed to pull out of the dive, with wings level, the height was insufficient for recovery and all died in the ensuing crash on the middle of the Blagnac airfield.

The resulting inquiry by a French military body within the Direction General d'Aviation (DGA) that investigates test flight accidents found that the accident was "a combination of several factors, not one of which, in isolation, would have caused the crash." The report highlighted slow crew response, poor coordination, and incorrect actions, and said the A330's speed needed to be monitored during autopilot/altitude capture operations. Airbus was also asked to reexamine its policy for test flight categories and who was permitted to be aboard. It was also told to ensure that test flight crews were to be systematically prepared for upcoming tests.

The investigation revealed that Warner had an extremely busy day, and before the A330 test flight, had already captained an A321 demonstration flight, supervised a simulator session, and attended two meetings. His busy schedule meant it was impossible to fit in a proper briefing for the crew—another vital mistake.

Crucially for Airbus, however, the inquiry exonerated the aircraft's basic systems and concluded that had the event happened at a greater altitude, the alpha-protect and alphas-floor functions would have tripped the autopilot and recovered the aircraft.

While Airbus recovered from the crash tragedy, work went on to clear the Trent-powered version for service. Tests had revealed a disappointing 2 percent shortfall in predicted fuel consumption, bringing the R-R engine in at 1.5 percent below its GE rival, and around 2.5 percent below P&W. Despite the problems, the mood was upbeat at the Farnborough air show that year when the first R-R test aircraft itself was proudly displayed in the new livery of Cathay Pacific Airways. At the show, Airbus chief executive Jean Pierson remarked that British engines made the A330 variant the most "European" of any Airbus to-date, a far cry from the bitter anti-British sentiments of former years.

Later in the same show, Airbus announced that the JAA had approved the PW4164/68-powered version for 90-minute ETOPS, further underlining the overall confidence in the program despite the miserable events of the previous six months.

Nonetheless these continued to haunt the program. The crash delayed certification of the aircraft's Cat 3 automatic landing system and both Thai and MAS refused to take delivery of their first aircraft until this had been achieved. Although this was finally approved by the DGA on October 28, 1994, deliveries were still held up while both Thai Airways International and MAS sought compensation for delays and deferrals, respectively.

These issues were finally resolved and Thai Airways International took delivery of its first A330 in December. The airline inaugurated commercial services with the aircraft on December 19, 1994, between Bangkok, Taipei, and Seoul. Malaysia Airlines, which had undergone a change in ownership the previous June, sought to defer delivery as long as it could. After leasing two MD-11s for an interim period, it finally accepted its first A330s in February 1995.

Within days of the MAS delivery, Cathay Pacific Airways also received its first Trent-powered A330s. The R-R version of the A330 had been certified on December 22, 1994, after completing more than 300 hours of flight testing. The airworthiness ticket covered the use of the baseline Trent 768-60, rated at 67,500 pounds thrust for the A330-341 version, as well as the 71,100-pound thrust Trent 772-60, selected by Cathay Pacific for its heavier A330-342 versions.

The predelivery tests also included a 120-hour route-proving exercise with Cathay Pacific, as well as a 3,000 simulated engine cycle ETOPS test by R-R as part of the effort to gain clearance for 60-minute ETOPS at entry-into-service. This was extended to 90-minutes ETOPS by midyear, and by 1996 had been increased to 120 minutes. This was expected to be the limit for Cathay Pacific, which planned to use the A330 as a replacement for L-1011 TriStars on regional routes within Asia.

By 1995, all three main versions of the A330 were in revenue service and from an operational perspective, Airbus's plan was on track. The marketing and sales story, on the other hand, was disappointing. Sales of medium-range wide-bodies had spent several years in the doldrums from the early 1990s, and the A330-300 was particularly hard hit. Airbus was determined to rejuvenate the twinjet and was about to develop a winning strategy.

CHAPTER SEVEN

VARIATIONS ON A THEME

n 1995 flagging sales of the A330-300 and growing concerns over the market penetration of the Boeing 767-300ER forced an unexpected change in the course of new A330 developments. Up until this time, Airbus had been focused on developing heavier-weight and increased-capacity versions. Earlier in 1995, however, its sales teams reported that airlines ideally wanted increased range and slightly less capacity. By April that year the consortium revealed plans to fill the mid-size wide-body niche with a shortened version of the A330.

Showers of sparks pour from the test tailskid beneath the aft fuse-lage of the A330-200 as it performs minimum unstick speed (Vmu) tests at dawn during a cold winter day at Toulouse in January 1998. *Airbus*

Known variously as the A329, A330M10, and finally the A330-200, the new version simply traded airframe weight for range at a fraction of the cost of an all-new development. Airbus concluded that a shrunken, 250-seater version of the –300 would cost around $450 million to develop, and would offer direct operating costs some 9 percent below those of the 767-300ER. It also estimated a potential market for around 800 aircraft in the market category over the 1995–2015 period, and believed it could offer a product by 1998 if launched by the end of 1995.

By aiming it at the 6,400 nautical miles range sector occupied so successfully by the 767, Airbus conceded that the longer-range twin concept was more viable than it had first thought. Part of this was due to continued improvements in engine performance, proven reliability, and a successful ETOPS track record. Another aspect was the spread of point-to-point long-haul services that followed deregulation in the

Previous Page: Despite the persistent reluctance of Airbus to venture into long-range twin territory, the immediate sales success of the A330-200 was apparent from the start—as witnessed by the numerous logos festooned on the side of this Rolls-Royce Trent-powered prototype. In all, Airbus forecasted a market demand for some 3,600 aircraft in the 250- to 300-seat range up to 2020, of which it conservatively estimated 800 would be taken up with A330-200 sales.

The structural upgrades developed for the heavier –300E variant of the A340, pictured in the foreground, provided the foundations for the launch of the A330-200, Airbus' answer to the Boeing 767-300ER. By July 1998, when this image was captured, the second A330-200 airframe (number 195) had been reengined with Rolls-Royce Trent 700s and is seen in the background.

United States, and a general easing of the tight bilateral air service agreements that governed international air travel, particularly across the North Atlantic.

Another was simply the market. Airlines wanted an alternative to the twin-engined 767-300ER, and Airbus was the only option. Confident of a revival in the A330 order book, the Airbus Industrie Supervisory Board approved the –200 development on November 24, 1995, and three days later the consortium officially gave the project the go-ahead. The reasons for going ahead were twofold: a new product to keep existing A300/A310 customers loyal, and a new generation

The foreshortened appearance of the A330-200, emphasized in this view, was a result of the removal of 10 fuselage frames. Overall length was therefore reduced to 191 feet 5 inches, while the fin and rudder were also extended by more than 3 feet to counter the reduced moment arm. Two-class capacity was lowered from 335 to 293, and three-class from 295 to 253.

replacement for the large fleets of aging DC-10-30s and Lockheed L-1011-200s and –500s in service.

The timing of the –200 actually hinged on plans to develop a higher-weight version of the A340 (see chapter 5). This was introduced as a "step change" from the A340-300, and was centered on the provision of a stronger wing and beefed-up wing/root join. The heavier A340-300E, as it was called, was offered with a maximum takeoff weight of more than 605,700 pounds and a range of almost 7,500 nautical miles. At the same time, Airbus outlined a similarly structured A340-200E, complete with auxiliary fuel tanks. Configured for 232 passengers, the aircraft boasted a potential range of 8,000 nautical miles. As a result, the proposed derivative was later renamed the A340-8000 (see chapter 8).

The A330-200 is often described as a "pilot's aircraft" and has spritely performance for a large transport. Handling characteristics are somewhat "tamed" by the fly-by-wire flight control system, which restricts some maneuvers to protect the airframe from being overstressed. The system automatically trims the aircraft for each flight condition, including turns at bank angles up to 33 degrees. The aircraft would therefore maintain this bank angle, should the crew take their hands off the side-stick, until further control inputs were made.

The emergence of the A330-200 provided powerful competition for Boeing's long range twin family, namely the 767 and 777—the –300 version of which is glimpsed here in close contact with the new Airbus at the Farnborough show in 1998. By 2001, the A330-200 had dealt a serious blow to Boeing's previous dominance with the 767, while the 777 had conversely dented the market potential of the A340.

The strengthened wing for the new A340 versions enabled the A330-200 takeoff weight to be increased to 506,600 pounds. Building on this development in turn, Airbus also planned to offer the strengthened wing on the A330–300. This was to increase the big twin's range to 7,500 nautical miles, with deliveries starting in 1999.

All this was in the future, however, as Airbus completed design work on the rejigged A330 through the winter of 1995 and early 1996. The basic changes included strengthening the wing with thicker gauge skins, and chopping out chunks of the fuselage to reduce two-class seating from 335 to 293, and three-class seating from 295 to 253. The length of the "chop" was "market driven," and aimed at finding the ideal compromise between capacity and range to suit the needs of as many airlines as possible. The longer the aircraft, the more it could seat but the shorter distances it would fly, and vice-versa.

The shortened A330 measured 193 feet 7 inches in length, some 15 feet less than its bigger brother. To offset the reduced moment arm of the shorter body, Airbus also added a 3 foot 5 inch extension to the tail fin giving the A330-200 an overall height of 58 feet 8 inches. The aircraft was otherwise dimensionally identical to the –300.

The fin tip extension involved the enlargement of the fin torsion box, as well as a 6 percent increase in the chord of the rudder. To cope with the increased loads of the bigger rudder Airbus replaced the three existing 20,900-pound independent, hydraulically activated servos with more powerful, 44,000-pound actuators. The larger rudder also had a +/- five degree increase in travel, to 35 degrees, which meant having to relocate the actuators. Instead of sitting parallel, relative to the chord of the rudder, they were set in diagonal positions.

Despite the taller fin, Airbus decided to delete the truss structure from the rear fuselage that originally was designed to support the tail unit. Instead, Airbus structural analysis suggested the torsion box would be adequately held by simply incorporating the fin's four support pickup points into the stressed skin and frame structure of the rear fuselage.

The shrink was obtained by removing 10 fuselage frames, four from the aft section and six from the forward fuselage. The four aft-most frames were removed from between doors three and four, and the forward frames from between door two and the wing. In the A340-200, which was similarly reduced by the removal of 10 frames, the forward section was modified by removing frames in the area between doors one and two. The reason for the difference between the two was that the shorter CFM56 engines of the A340 did not obstruct access to door two, while the larger engines on the A330 would have presented some problems.

It took more than a simple reduction in structural weight to increase range, and fuel capacity was substantially aug-

To boost the marketing strength of the A330-200, Airbus traded fuselage weight for range, and activated the center fuselage fuel tank. The result was a much greater fuel capacity of 36,750 U.S. gallons, compared to 25,760 U.S. gallons in the A330-300. Range with full load went up to 6,650 nautical miles, a full 1,000 nautical miles longer than the larger version.

mented in the –200 to guarantee intercontinental ranges. Capacity was boosted to 36,700 U.S. gallons (139,100 liters) by activating the center section fuel tank that was standard on the A340. The aircraft also incorporated the A330/A340's standard tailplane trim fuel tank.

Aerospatiale began final assembly of the first A330-200 at Toulouse early in 1997, with the mating of the forward, center, and aft fuselage sections taking place on March 25. The following month, the tail fin was delivered from Dasa Airbus' (the former Deutsche Airbus) Stade facility near Hamburg, and systems checks were underway around late April.

By this stage, thanks to the advent of the –200, the A330 order book was looking healthy once more. International Lease Finance Corporation had started the ball rolling with a firm order for 13 in March 1996, and by June 1997 the order tally had reached 85 from 8 customers. These included Asiana, Austrian Airlines, Emirates, Sabena, and Swissair. Air-

bus also upped its market forecast saying the demand for aircraft in the 250-300-seat category was in the 3,000 range over the next 20 years.

At last, on August 13, the first A330-200 made its maiden flight commanded by Airbus chief test pilot, William Wainwright. Along with test pilot Bernard Schafer, and flight test engineers Jacky Joye, Roger Lignee, and Jean Marie Mathios, Wainwright took the aircraft to its maximum altitude of 41,000 feet and flew it in basic and normal control modes. Some basic tests at low-speed and high-speed configurations were also carried out without encountering any problems.

International Lease Finance Corporation, as launch customer, had chosen GE engines, and the prototype therefore flew with the CF6-80E1A4 version of the big fan. The test program, which like that of the –300 version was designed to encompass all three of the big fan engines, was set to last 16 months and involve around 630 flight test hours. The second test development aircraft, powered by P&W engines, was destined to join the effort in December 1997, with certification expected the following May.

The first aircraft retrofitted with the Rolls-Royce Trent 700 engines and flight tests were scheduled to begin with this combination in March 1998, with certification expected the following December. Total orders, options, and commitments for the new variant had climbed to 132 by this stage and Airbus predicted eventual A330-200 sales of between 500 and 600 aircraft over the next 20 years.

While the A330-200 was coming to life, Airbus was busy tackling worrying in-service issues that dogged both the A330 and A340. One of the most serious was a series of hydraulic pump fires that left at least two aircraft badly damaged, and was the suspected cause of another fire that completely destroyed an Air France A340 on the ground in January 1994.

Problems got so bad that by January 1997, Airbus instructed all operators to deactivate the electrically driven pumps. The alert bulletin followed a serious fire on a MAS A330-300 that had been undergoing a routine overnight line check at Singapore's Changi airport on January 4 that year.

The fire, which was suspected as having started in an overheated pump in the right-hand main landing gear wheel well, caused around $30 million of damage that took about six months to repair.

The problem, which had also resulted in a similar blaze on an Air Mauritius A340-300 during routine maintenance the previous October, was traced to three Vickers hydraulic-electrical pumps. These were used as in-flight backups to the engine-driven pumps that worked the yellow, green, and blue hydraulic systems. The yellow electrical pump, located in the forward bulkhead of the right main wheel well, was also used on the ground to work the cargo doors. Airlines immediately discontinued using the pumps and began opening and closing doors manually until a solution was found. Airbus meanwhile began looking at alternative pumps.

That year also saw a series of in-flight shutdowns of Rolls-Royce Trent 700 engines that caused this version of the A330-300 to have its hard-won ETOPS clearances temporarily suspended. Problems first cropped up in November 1996 when a Cathay Pacific flight returned to Hong Kong with an engine shut down. Associate carrier Dragonair also suffered a Trent 700 failure on April 17, 1997, caused by carbon clogging an

Extending 197 feet 10 inches from tip to tip, the elegantly designed A330 wing has a sweep of 30 degrees and an aspect ratio of 9.3. Thickness-to-chord ratio varies from 15.25 percent at the deep root of the wing, to 10.6 percent at the tip. The trailing edge also features two kink points marking the break point between the inboard and outboard flaps and the outboard ailerons.

oil filter. Cathay then suspended its own 120-minute ETOPS clearance, which the Hong Kong Civil Aviation Department later made official.

A few weeks later, on May 6, trouble struck the A330 fleet again when a Cathay aircraft suffered another failure on climb-out from Hong Kong. The trouble was traced to the step-aside gearbox mounted outside of the core engine. The Hispano-Suiza–built gearbox had suffered a bearing failure, though the cause remained unclear.

On May 9, another Cathay A330 was climbing out of Bangkok en route to Hong Kong, when oil pressure in one engine suddenly dropped and the engine began to spool down. The crew was forced to return to Bangkok on the remaining engine, and discovered after landing that the engine's master chip detector showed metal contamination. The problems continued with a fifth in-flight engine failure on May 23, forcing both Cathay and Dragonair to voluntarily ground their combined fleet of 15 A330-300s the following day.

The grounding caused massive disruption as Cathay's 11 aircraft accounted for 17 percent of the fleet and 15 percent of its seat capacity. Dragonair, which relied on the big twins to operate its busy trunk route to Beijing, Kaohsiung, and Shanghai, was in a similar fix. For Cathay the grounding could not have come at a worse time. This was the busiest time in the airline's history as the United Kingdom prepared to hand back the territorial possession of Hong Kong to the Chinese at the end of June 1997.

Rolls-Royce and Hispano-Suiza feverishly worked on a solution and by June had devised a better system for lubricating the trouble-spot—the driving-shaft locator ball-bearing. Insufficient lubrication had resulted in premature fatigue, overheating, and, finally, failure of the bearing. A redesigned lubrication system was dispatched to the fleet and the problem vanished as quickly as it had emerged.

Other issues continued to hound the engine, however, including surge, vibration, and turbine disc erosion problems. At least three surges were experienced in service because of excess clearances in the second stage high compressor. The cure involved respraying the lining of the compressor with a new material. Vibration problems, centered on the high-pressure turbine (HPT) module, were rectified by changing the material of the retaining bolts to the same as that of the compressor and turbine discs.

The HPT erosion issue was traced to moisture getting into the turbine blade air-cooling system. This resulted in a

The large undercarriage appears to reach for the runway as this Gulf Air A330-200 nears touchdown. Despite the weight increase, the –200 does not feature the center main leg of the A340, allowing the space to be used for extra fuel instead.

drastic reduction in fatigue life from around 15,000 cycles to 5,000 cycles and was tackled by redesigning parts of the cooling system to reduce moisture levels.

Hot on the heels of the Trent engine crisis came more problems for Airbus in Asia. Prompted by a financial crisis in Japan, the entire region suffered an economic "meltdown" and

by early 1998 all the "tiger" economies were in trouble. Amongst the hardest hit was South Korea, and with it Asian Airlines, a leading A330 customer. In late January 1998, it scrapped plans to buy 18 A330-200/300s as part of drastic measures to survive the downturn then engulfing the country. Neighboring Thai Airways International was similarly afflicted and requested deferrals on 11 Airbus orders, including three A330-200s and five A300-600Rs.

Overall, however, it was Boeing and not Airbus that was most badly hit by the "Asian flu" as it was nicknamed. In early 1998, a much larger proportion of the more expensive wide-bodies under threat of cancellation or deferral was Boeing 747-400s (48) and 777s (93). This accounted for almost 35 percent of the backlog for these types. By contrast, the Airbus backlog at the time included only 40 outstanding A330/A340s in the region, or around 17 percent.

The news was cheering for Airbus, which had just begun celebrating its best year ever. Its net order tally for 1997 was 438 aircraft, some 20 higher than its previous boom year of 1989. More importantly, perhaps, its bulging order book

Airbus had taken 675 total sales for the A330/A340 family by the start of 2001, claiming 53 percent share of the hotly contested market for the year 2000, and a 55 percent market share overall. Newcomers to the fold included SAS and Qantas, though stalwart Airbus customers like Austrian, Cathay Pacific Airways, Lufthansa, and Thai Airways International continued to bring business. By 2001, Austrian had five A330s in service, Cathay had more than 30 A330/A340s on order or in service, and Lufthansa had ordered 49 A340s, 32 of which had been delivered. Thai Airways International had 12 A330s in service by this stage.

represented 45 percent of new business in terms of units and a little over 40 percent of the dollar value. Airbus had actually drawn level with Boeing three years earlier, but that had been during the bad years when none of the order tallies were particularly impressive; 1997 was different.

As if to underscore the consortium's new-found resilience, the bad news from Asia was almost immediately balanced by stronger sales elsewhere. Air Lanka, the national airline of Sri Lanka, ordered six A330-200s in March that year, after Emirates agreed to take a 40 percent stake in the carrier. The A330s were to replace L-1011-500s, fulfilling Airbus' original dreams for the big twin. Air Lanka further underlined the consortium's sense of planning by confirming cockpit commonality with the A340 as another major reason for selecting the A330. The new aircraft would also be common with the 16 Rolls-Royce Trent-powered A330-200s recently ordered by Emirates.

At the end of March, Airbus also received simultaneous JAA, FAA, and Transport Canada certification for the GE CF6-powered A330-200. The ticket was awarded after 380 hours of flight testing, clearing the way for what all hoped would be a trouble-free introduction into service with Canada 3000 in April. Unfortunately, this was not to be, for on its inaugural flight from Toronto to Vancouver, the aircraft was forced to divert to Winnipeg because of an engine problem.

Although somewhat embarrassing, the precautionary diversion was caused by an indication of low oil pressure in one engine. This was traced to an oil leak in the "D-sump" around the number four bearing area. General Electric inspected the problem area and redesigned the affected parts.

It is not known if this incident helped in any way to sway US Airways towards P&W, which it subsequently selected to power a fleet of A330-200s that Airbus announced as a landmark order in July 1998. By ordering the big twin, US Airways became the first American carrier to operate any of the new generation Airbus wide-bodies. While both TWA and Northwest had long-standing orders for the A330, both airlines had deferred deliveries indefinitely. It was not until 2001, that Northwest finally firmed up plans to buy the A330.

The deal for up to 30 aircraft was won after a hotly contested battle with Boeing competing with the 767-300/400. Although Boeing was "not far behind" in its bid, the airline said the Airbus twinjet offered "more capacity for passengers and cargo, more range, more passenger appeal, and better delivery positions." Although it did not, perhaps, represent the historical significance for Airbus of the Eastern A300 or Northwest A320 order, the US Airways deal nonetheless spoke volumes for the credibility of Airbus and the A330-200 in particular.

The spread of longer range Airbus twin operations around the world is typified by the magnificent sight of this Corsair-operated A330-200 landing at the Caribbean resort island of St. Maarten. Average flight sector times for the A330-200 were similar to the A340 at between 3.5 and 8 hours in 2000, compared to between 1.7 and 3.5 hours for the A330-300. The worldwide A330-200 fleet was also recording a dispatch reliability (departing within 15 minutes of schedule) of 98.9 percent by the start of the century.

The American operator also selected an unusual engine for its new twin, the P&W PW4173. This was a hybrid combining the 100-inch diameter fan of the PW4164/68 engine already used on the A330, with a higher thrust core recently developed for the PW4098 engine used on the stretched Boeing 777-300. As it turned out, airlines were put off by the risk of the project and without US Airways ever firming up its selection, the PW4173 plan was dropped after orders for just three shipsets were taken.

Within months of the US Airways order, Airbus suffered a setback after an A340-200 suffered an undercarriage collapse at Brussels Airport, Belgium. The incident occurred as a Sabena aircraft arrived in from New York on August 29, 1998. After what appeared to be a routine landing, the starboard main gear failed near the end of the runway, followed seconds later by the central gear. Sagging down on one side, the right wingtip and engines scraped the ground and the aircraft rotated through almost 100 degrees, following which there was an emergency evacuation of the 255 passengers and 10 crew on board.

Investigation revealed the two-wheel rear section of the right main bogey had separated, and the main gear barrel had broken near the retraction actuator. Airbus immediately issued instructions to all operators to check all A330 and A340 gears after 800 flight cycles, and every 120 cycles thereafter. It also limited the turning radius of both aircraft types until a fix could be found.

The gear manufacturer, Messier-Dowty, meanwhile worked on a permanent fix to the problem that was traced to excess stress in the torque link in the upper part of the gear. The solution turned out to be the removal of "a small amount of metal" from the torque link, to eliminate the stress point, plus additional strengthening of the center gear leg.

Certification of the Rolls-Royce Trent 700-powered A330-200, meanwhile, was completed by March 1999 following a six-month flight test program involving more than 75 flights and 200 engine running-hours. First deliveries commenced shortly after, with Montreal-based Air Transat of Canada taking the initial aircraft on lease from ILFC. The charter company put the long-haul A330 into service on a network of new routes to Hawaii, Frankfurt, and Athens. In later service, Canada 3000 also flew the twin to Fiji, Sydney, Auckland, and the Cook Islands, exploiting its ETOPS capabilities to the fullest.

Two months later it was the A340's turn to mark a milestone in the history of Airbus when a −300 model became the

Hong Kong-based Dragonair was operating five A330s by 2001, having recovered from a crisis period in 1997 when its entire fleet was temporarily grounded because of problems with a gearbox on its aircrafts' Rolls-Royce Trent engines.

Monarch was among a growing band of charter operators of the A330-200. Together with fellow charter carrier Canada 3000, Monarch had the hardest working fleets by 2000, operating its aircraft for up to 15 hours a day. The A330-200 fleet, by this stage, was showing an hours-to-cycles (complete flights from takeoff to landing) ratio of 4:1, compared to 2.2:1 for the A330-300. Monarch chose the A330-200 over the 767-300ER, and secondhand DC-10s because of prospects for higher long-term residual values.

2,000th aircraft to be delivered by the consortium. The aircraft was, fittingly, delivered to Lufthansa, which by this stage was Airbus' largest single airline customer. The event marked a spectacular ramp-up in productivity for the consortium that had taken 15 years to achieve its 500th delivery in June 1989. Four more years elapsed until the 1,000th shipment, in March 1993, and another four years passed before the 1,500th came in February 1997. From then it had taken just two years to get to the 2,000th and, based on its bulging backlog of 1,300 orders, Airbus predicted it would hit the 3,000th delivery in 2002.

Work also continued to keep the A330 and A340 families fully competitive and up-to-date. This ranged from flight tests of a new, Honeywell-built Pegasus flight management system (FMS) in the A340, to studying bigger engines for heavier A330 variants, and updated engines for improved A340 versions.

The plan to revitalize the A340 was first revealed by CFM in February 2000 when it acknowledged studies to combine the CFM56-5C with the core of the –5B/P. "There is a need to improve the exhaust gas temperature margin on that engine," said CFM president Gerard Laviec. He added the plan would improve operating margin, boost hot-and-high payload, and cut maintenance costs. The –5B/P engine had

been developed in the mid-1990s for the A320 family, and included three-dimensional aerodynamic design in the HP compressor. This was also featured in another subsequent engine, the –7B, developed for the Next Generation 737.

Airbus and CFM revealed the upgrade officially at Farnborough 2000. The aircraft was dubbed the A340 Enhanced and was to be made available from 2003, with the engine upgrade kit to be offered as a retrofit option to existing operators from late 2003 onward.

While maintaining the competitive edge of the A330 and A340 remained a priority, another focus for activity was the development of newer family members to replace earlier A300s and A310s. One of the likeliest of these emerged in 1999 as a proposed derivative called the A330M19. The study was a nine-frame fuselage shrink of the A330-200, itself a nine-frame shrink of the –300. As a result, the project was nicknamed externally the A330-100, but internally was referred to by the designation A306. However, it would eventually be dubbed the –500. The 200-seat aircraft was targeted at a maximum takeoff weight of 480,000 pounds and a range of up to 6,400 nautical miles. It was to be powered by 60,000-pound thrust engines that were widely expected to be de-rated versions of the current A330 powerplants.

Brazilian airline TAM is among the increasingly diverse A330 operator group, operating five on routes to Europe and the United States as well as domestically between Sao Paulo, Recife, and Fortaleza. The first of five aircraft was finally delivered in late 1998 after hold-ups caused by the Brazilian currency crisis in 1997. TAM's fleet was previously made up entirely of small Fokker F27 and F50 turboprops and Fokker 100 jetliners. In 1998, TAM also ordered 38 A320 family aircraft, almost half of which had been delivered by 2001.

An upgraded A340-300 version, dubbed the –300 Enhanced, was announced at the 2000 Farnborough show. The bulk of the improvements, which were to be certified for entry into service in 2003, were centered on engine improvements. These were meant to counter nagging maintenance problems and slightly higher than anticipated in-flight shut down rates of 0.007 per 1,000 flying hours. Some features were meant for retrofit and offered to large A340 customers, including Lufthansa, one of whose aircraft is seen in late evening at the Farnborough show.

CFM International's CFM56-5C development program committed in 2000 to produce a 1.1 percent improvement in fuel consumption and a 13 degree centigrade exhaust gas temperature reduction. The result was expected to be quieter, more reliable engines with lower maintenance costs. The modified –5C included improved three-dimensional aerodynamic design features in the compressor and turbine, both taken from the –5B/P engine developed for the A320 family. The first revised engine began tests in late 2001.

One possible outsider under consideration was a geared fan proposal from P&W called the PW8160. This advanced concept was also being proposed for the A340-500/600 program, (see chapter 8), and the shrink A330 would therefore have given P&W an extra application for the same basic engine.

The modular approach used aspects of the different branches of the A330 family and made sense to Airbus. But it did not go down well with some operators that worried about carrying around excess structural weight that resulted from this approach. By early 2000, Airbus responded by reconfiguring the study with an advanced wing based on the A300-600, and by incorporating A330 structural and system features.

By March 2000, Airbus announced it was accelerating the new derivative study with a proposed entry-into-service date of 2003. The move was prompted by increasing airline interest in a new 200 to 250-seat wide-body, particularly Singapore which was hunting for an A310 fleet replacement. The aircraft was expected to have "at least 5 percent" better specific fuel consumption than the A300-600, and by now was offered with study engines called the CF6-80G2, the PW4000, and the Trent 500.

In the buildup to the Farnborough air show that year, at which the formal launch of the project was by now widely expected, Airbus extended the study to include at least three versions. The baseline A330-100 was to have a range of 4,500 nautical miles, while a second longer-range variant with the capability to fly 6,700 nautical miles was outlined to cater to European–U.S. West Coast routes. A third version, tied specifically to the requirements of prospective launch customer ILFC, was designed to have a greater maximum takeoff weight and a range in excess of 7,000 nautical miles.

As it turned out, the Farnborough show did not provide the platform for the launch of the A330-500, as it was by now formally called by Airbus. Instead, details emerged of new studies to once again grow the A330-300 to rival the 777. Dubbed the –300HGW (high gross weight), the proposed aircraft had a maximum weight of almost 530,000 pounds, more powerful engines, and increased fuel capacity to 36,700 U.S. gallons. The extra fuel capacity was to be achieved by adopting the center section tank of the A330-200/A340, which was dry on the –300.

Once again ILFC appeared to be the main driver behind the development, which also emerged as a potential twin application for the GE-P&W Engine Alliance GP7000 in development for the A380 and soon-to-be-abandoned 747X. However, it was the launch of the A380, combined with the parallel development of both the A340-500/600 and A318, that curtailed the A330-500 and A330HGW efforts.

Despite this, not all efforts on new A330 derivatives ceased. The surging cargo market, that would sustain the A300-600F production line well into the first decade twenty-first century, also provided a valuable new opportunity for its big twin derivative. Studies of a freighter derivative of the A330-200F proved so attractive that first deliveries were initially set for as early as 2004. The new freighter was designed with a 130,000-pound payload capacity and a range of more than 4,000 nautical miles. With 15 percent more payload than the A300-600Fand double the range, it seemed only a matter of time before Airbus would begin writing the next chapter of its big twin success story.

CHAPTER EIGHT

THE FINAL STRETCH

The astonishing sight of the A340-600 taking to the air on its maiden flight on April 23, 2001, was a decade in the making.

In the early days of 1991, Airbus began simple stretch studies of its A340-300 under the name A340-400X. These had been prompted by Boeing's launch of the 777 and with it a family plan that could threaten the long-term future of the European jetliner. Four years earlier it had been Airbus' turn to catch Boeing and McDonnell Douglas apparently off-guard by

launching the big quad jet—the first all-new, long-range wide-body for a generation. McDonnell Douglas had responded with the MD-11 while Boeing came back in 1990 with the highly impressive 777.

Now it was once more the turn of Airbus to respond with stretch studies that revolved around the inevitable demand for more range and payload. They were also aimed at the 747 replacement market, something Airbus would hardly dreamed of being capable of just a few years before. Aside from the fundamental question about how large to make the new version, the study team debate raged to and fro about one key factor above all other—that of engine power.

Right from the start Airbus realized the CFM56 could only take the A340 family so far into the future. Based on the original –400X studies of 1991, a 12-frame (20 feet 7 inch) stretch version seating 340 in three classes would have been penalized in range by as much as 1,500 nautical miles using

Virgin Atlantic Airways helped launch the stretch A340 program in September 1997, when it signed for 10 aircraft and 8 options. The British airline intended to use the –600s to partly replace five Boeing 747-200s, as well as for expansion. This aircraft, pictured in the carrier's new 2000 livery, is actually the second A340-300 prototype, which performed five years' worth of testing for Airbus before being refurbished and handed over to Virgin in May 1997. Virgin also operates the third A340-300 prototype.

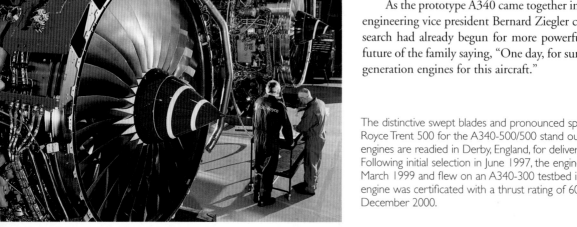

the existing wings and engines. In response, Airbus began asking the engine makers for proposals for a larger new engine in the 40,000- to 45,000-pound thrust class.

As the prototype A340 came together in Toulouse, Airbus engineering vice president Bernard Ziegler confirmed that the search had already begun for more powerful engines for the future of the family saying, "One day, for sure, we'll have new-generation engines for this aircraft."

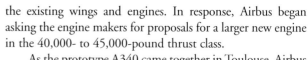

The distinctive swept blades and pronounced spinners of the Rolls-Royce Trent 500 for the A340-500/500 stand out as the first batch of engines are readied in Derby, England, for delivery to Toulouse. Following initial selection in June 1997, the engine made its first run in March 1999 and flew on an A340-300 testbed in June 2000. The engine was certificated with a thrust rating of 60,000 pounds in December 2000.

During May 1991, Airbus duly received proposals from both R-R and P&W, both of which were anxious to gain a foothold. The British engine maker put forward a new concept based on the ACCORD (advanced civil core demonstrator), funded by the U.K. Ministry of Defence. It also offered a lighter weight version of the RB.211-535E4, which powered the 757, and indeed this appeared to be a more likely candidate. Pratt & Whitney similarly offered a new variant of its 757 engine, dubbed the PW2136, as well as a more revolutionary engine based on its ultra high-bypass Advanced Ducted Prop (ADP) concept.

CFM was not going to take the challenge lying down and in November 1991 announced it was planning a new engine, termed the CFMXX, targeted at the mid-thrust level between the CFM56 and the GE90. CFM chairman Jean Bilien said the engine would cost between $1.0 and $1.5 billion to develop, adding, "If there is a market for the new engine, as we think there will be a market for the A340 stretched and other similar sized aircraft, financing to develop it will be forthcoming."

By the following year the three main engine options were entrenched, with P&W's ADP appearing to be in the lead. Rolls-Royce meanwhile described its meetings with Airbus as "routine in terms of discussing the aircraft and what we can provide by way of an engine to match. One thing is for certain, it will be a –535 derivative," R-R confidently added. Only history would prove how wrong this was.

The next three years saw a lull in A340-400X studies as recession swept through the industry and Airbus concentrated on introducing the baseline A330/A340 into service. By 1995 the market was showing signs of revival and Airbus held the first of a series of customer focus group meetings. These meetings generated numerous suggestions, the most important of which was a larger, 20-frame stretch.

In October of that year, Airbus met with engine makers in St. Petersburg, Russia, and once more heard proposals to power the future stretch. CFM was in a far more bullish mood than before and argued that the stretched A340 market was too small to warrant an engine choice. In return for an estimated $2 billion commitment to develop the CFMXX, now rated at between 40,000- and 45,000-pounds thrust, it wanted exclusivity. Pratt & Whitney also argued the same, while R-R's attitude was more laissez-faire.

The full 245-foot, 11-inch length of the A340-600 is readily apparent from this side view, captured at the 2001 Paris Air Show. Compared with the –300, the –600 incorporates a 10-frame fuselage plug forward of the wing and a single frame extension just over the wing's leading edge. It also includes a three-frame fuselage plug and wing box extension, situated roughly between the words "quieter" and "smoother," and a six-frame extension aft of the trailing edge. The result of all this is a 34-foot, 10-inch stretch over the A340-300, and the world's longest airliner

The first aircraft, Serial Number 360, launched the flight test effort on April 23, 2001, with a 5-hour, 22-minute maiden flight from Toulouse, and took its first break from the planned 1,600-hour program to appear at the Paris show in June 2001. It was joined by two more –600 test aircraft during the year, and in February 2002 was due to be accompanied by the first –500. The A340-500 was scheduled to complete a 340-hour flight certification test effort by September 2002.

The massive main Messier-Dowty-built landing gear, which includes a four-wheel center gear for the first time on any Airbus aircraft, was one of 12 key "maturity" targets identified from the outset of the program. Others included the cabin, cargo loading system, electrical generation, flight controls, hydraulics, structure, built-in test and on-board maintenance, fuel system, bleed-air, powerplant, and lower-deck systems. Airbus hoped that by focusing on each target well ahead of actual service entry, the reliability of the A340-500/600 would be second to none. More than 500 "significant" improvements were made to the maturity targets as a result of this approach.

By early 1996 the pace began picking up. Airbus held another customer focus group meeting and gave the –400X a new name—the A340-600. At the same time, BAe made an important decision about the wing design of the new jet. Initial studies had focused on simple trailing edge modifications that, although they increased lift, did not provide much room for extra fuel. The company then studied a root extension, similar to the design used by McDonnell Douglas when it changed the DC-9 wing to meet the MD-80 requirements.

The winning solution, however, turned out to be a more subtle change called a tapered insert. Just as it sounds, this involved building into the wing a wedge-shaped insert that was 5 feet 3 inches wide (three frames) at the root and only a few inches wide by the time it got to the wingtip. The tip itself was also extended by more than five feet, along with the existing canted winglet. The modification increased wing area by 20 percent and, combined with the larger wing box resulting from the root insert, boosted fuel capacity by 38 percent.

Just as importantly, the design provided these benefits while enabling the leading and trailing edge components to be common with the existing A340 wing. The tip extension did require a longer seventh slat, but other changes were negligible. The overall wing sweep angle was increased from 30 degrees to 31.5 degrees as a result of the tapered insert and this, added to the increase in chord, was expected to yield a slight—but very welcomed—increase in cruise speed.

The overall span of the new aircraft would be 207 feet 5 inches, making it just a few feet short of the 747-400 span and easily the largest ever produced for a civil aircraft in Europe.

While BAe came up with its wing design breakthrough, wrangling continued over the engines. This came to a sudden and unexpected halt in April 1996 when GE signed a six-month exclusive deal with Airbus to study a power plant for the A340-600. The shock announcement covered the development of a new or derivative 51,000-pound thrust engine for what was now a 375-passenger, 7,000 nautical miles range aircraft.

What was most startling about the news was that CFM was suddenly left out in the cold. SNECMA, GE's partner in CFM, had been advocating the CFMXX and had wanted to lead the development by designing the high-pressure section of the engine. Until then SNECMA had been responsible for the low-pressure sections of all CFM engines, and GE had simply refused the request. The impasse killed the CFMXX dead and had serious implications for the Franco-American engine partnership.

The Trent 500, designated by the Rolls-Royce insignia on the nacelle, is the first UK-made engine to power an Airbus from entry into service. It paves the way for the Trent 900, which will be the first engine type to power the A380, in late 2004. The Trent 500 is a scaled-down version of the Trent 800, powering the Boeing 777, but it uses the smaller-diameter fan of the Trent 700, which powers the A330. In ground tests the Trent 500 reached around 68,000 pounds of thrust, though in service it will operate at 53,000 pounds on the A340-500 and at 56,000 pounds on the larger stretch.

The picture was even more complex because GE and SNECMA had also been in disagreement over the pricing of the GE90, while SNECMA had been at loggerheads with Airbus in a similar dispute about the price of the CFM56. SNECMA president Bernard Dufour had refused to lower CFM56 prices, making it more difficult for Airbus to sell the A340 against the 777, where a cut-throat competition between the Big Three engine makers had brought low prices and big wins for Boeing. The effect was so dramatic that ebullient Airbus chief executive Jean Pierson had even gone so far as to say SNECMA was, "killing the A340."

Ironically, in later years the long-term affect of the GE-SNECMA dispute was a two-year hiatus in GE90 development. This had a knock-on effect in delaying the ultra-long haul 777X, an arch rival of the new A340 versions, thereby aiding the Airbus marketing campaign in the long run.

In May 1996, the latest focus group meeting came up with a profound change in direction for the fledgling program. Why not, they asked, combine the new wings and engines of the "super stretch" –600 with the fuselage of the –300 to produce a super-long range version? The move would certainly help Airbus provide a ready solution to the emerging ultra-long-range market and provide a much better answer than the heavily compromised A340-8000.

This had been configured with the strengthened –300E wing, had a heavier takeoff weight of 606,300 pounds, and a "thrust bump" on the CFM56 engines. It was also 14 feet shorter than the standard –300 as part of the overall effort to trade weight for range. Despite being offered from 1994 onward, only Air Canada had expressed an interest in the version. Just before the 1996 focus meeting, Air Canada dropped its commitments for two A340-8000s saying they were too small.

The airline's executive vice president, Robert Milton said, "Once we studied the numbers there was no way we were ordering the aircraft as it stands." The aircraft was simply, "not big enough for it to be economical on Air Canada routes over those ranges," added Air Canada president Lamar Durrett.

Air Canada's decision was the death knell of the A340-8000, and only one of which was actually built for the Sultan of Brunei. It also spurred Airbus into launching the new hybrid, dubbed the A340-500. The designation A340-400 was reserved for a more modest "standby" stretch of the A340-300 capable of ranges of 6,100 nautical miles. Although this remained under study, the focus was firmly fixed on the –500/600, and by September the –400 had been dropped.

To keep structural empty weight as low as possible, Airbus introduced as much composite material and lighter-weight alloy as it could into the A340-500/600. Titanium is used in both the landing gear and engine mounting pylons, while the Aircell-made engine nacelles are made from impregnated carbon composites. This material is also used in the aft pressurization bulkhead and belly fairings, while the use of advanced aluminum alloys and thermoplastics in paneling and tubing helps save more than 2,500 pounds.

Despite being based on the original –300-size fuselage, the larger wing box meant the A340-500 was two fuselage frames longer and could therefore carry up to 310 passengers. Development costs for the new variants were set at "no less than $1 billion," according to Airbus chief operating officer Volker von Tein.

The following month, June 1996, SNECMA chief Dufour was ousted by the French government and replaced by Jean-Paul Bechat. The move was intended to thaw the frosty relations with GE, and revive the chances of French involvement in the A340-500/600 engine. Relations were subsequently "much improved," though uncertainty continued to surround both the size of the final thrust requirement and even the very launch of the airframe itself.

October brought good news for the program when MDC canceled plans to develop its proposed MD-11 rewinged, stretch derivative, the MD-XX. The aircraft, if launched, would have provided stiff opposition to both the A340-600 and 777X and was being seriously considered by American Airlines and Swissair when the ax fell. The move also put to rest any last chances of reviving the fortunes of the baseline MD-11, aiding both Airbus and Boeing, the latter of which was to acquire the ailing company the next year.

Talks with GE meanwhile reached new levels of intensity as the six-month exclusivity agreement neared its end. Talks centered on a new, very high-bypass ratio turbofan in the 55,000- to 60,000-pound thrust class. Although the "GEXX" engine was described as a "very exciting" prospect by Airbus senior vice president for strategic planning, Adam Brown, the talks remained bogged down by "significant economic issues."

At stake was the proposed development time scale for the big new jets that was aimed at a 2001 in-service date. General Electric remained worried about the overall market size, while Airbus remained convinced it would sell up to 600 of the $130 million priced A340-500/600.

Amid the continuing uncertainty R-R revealed in February 1997 plans to develop a shrink version of the Trent aimed at the thrust range needed by the new Airbus. Speaking in London, the engine maker's chairman Sir Ralph Robins said, "A smaller core [than that of the Trent 900], also scaled from the Trent 800 but using the Trent 700 fan, would produce a very exciting engine."

Only days after Sir Ralph's comments, talks between Airbus and GE broke down. General Electric blamed the failure on the inability of the two sides "to agree on financial terms

The BAE Systems-designed wing is 20 per cent larger in area, enabling up to 11,760 gallons of extra fuel to be stored, compared with the A340-300. Additional wing area created by the tapered root insert increases the overall lift capacity of the aircraft by 40 per cent and helps give a greatly improved initial climb and cruise altitude capability. At the start of the test effort, early performance figures showed the A340-600 capable of climbing to 33,000 feet in no more than 38 minutes and 178 nautical miles, compared with 70 minutes and roughly double the distance for a 777-300ER.

and conditions. We defined the engine for the aircraft's technical requirements, but could not reach agreement on price and risk-sharing." The lack of a second airframe application also clouded GE's vision of the proposed $1 billion-plus development effort.

Airbus vowed to try and stick to its original 2001 target despite the collapse of the GE deal. Attention switched to R-R and P&W, the latter again proposing its ADP as well as a low-risk option called the PW4557 based on existing technology. Rolls-Royce meanwhile put together what was described as an "extremely attractive" engineering and financial package to support its "shrink" Trent bid. Part of R-R's advantage was the extensive use of existing Trent technology in the proposed new engine, thereby cutting overall development costs and risks.

Amid mounting signs that R-R was onto a winner, news broke in March 1997 that SNECMA was negotiating with the British engine maker for a 25 percent share in the program. Just a year earlier, SNECMA president Bechat had turned down a R-R offer to join the Trent 900 effort saying its "natural loyalties" were with GE. Wind tunnel tests of the new wing at Farnborough, meanwhile, convinced Airbus senior vice president engineering, Alain Garcia, that the A340-500/600's performance would be, ". . . much greater than expected, with better lift capability and speed flexibility."

The results encouraged Airbus to begin sketching out growth plans for both versions with 10 percent more powerful engines, higher operating weights, and extra fuel for 500 nautical miles of additional range. The baseline –500 was, by this stage, configured to carry 313 passengers over 8,300 nautical miles and was to be powered by 53,000-pound thrust engines. The –600 was configured to seat 378 passengers, but had 1,000 nautical miles less range and required 55,950-pound thrust engines.

Finally, at the Paris air show in June 1997, Airbus signed a nonexclusive deal with R-R for the supply of what was now called the Trent 500 engine for the A340-500/600. Airbus said the deal provided "the best global package for our customers in terms of price and performance." It claimed the engine's predicted fuel consumption would be 7.7 percent lower than the Trent 700, helping the A340-600 to achieve 10 percent lower operating costs per seat than the A340-300 and 3 percent lower than the twin-engined 777-300X.

Although the deal with R-R left the door theoretically open to P&W as a second engine supplier in later years, it was effectively an exclusive deal as the option would not be made available until the 501st aircraft. Pratt & Whitney president Karl Krapek appeared resigned at the show saying, "Even with exclusivity, we would be well into a 23-year payback and would be $1.5 billion out of pocket. We decided to give R-R exclusivity. We won technically, we had

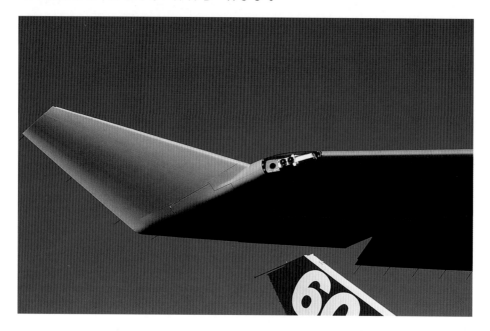

These detachable winglets are more sharply raked than the −300s, being set at an angle of 31.5 degrees, versus 29.7 degrees for the earlier version. Other changes to the wing include a manufacturing improvement that saved around 2,200 pounds in structural weight. Extra long billets of aluminum, previously unavailable to any manufacturer, were used for the first time on the A340-600 wing. This enabled BAE Systems to remove a large wing joint at the 62 per cent semispan position, cutting both structural weight and complication.

a lighter weight, lower fuel burn, and a year's advantage on service-entry." Pratt & Whitney's deal was based on a sales price of $2 million per engine for the first 50 aircraft and $3.7 million thereafter.

Airbus meanwhile revealed detailed changes to the configuration as it announced the commercial launch of the A340-500/600 at the show. It still remained shy of commitment to the long-awaited industrial launch, however. Flyaway price had increased to about $150 million, but with a claimed 15 percent lower trip cost than the 747-400 and a 60 percent greater cargo capacity. Conceding that the protracted engine selection process had impacted the time scale, Airbus also revealed that entry-into-service target was now 2002.

Both aircraft would also feature a new Messier-Dowty steerable center, four-wheeled landing gear as well as modified main and nose gears. The center gear was revised to retract forward instead of aft, freeing space for two additional freight pallets in the rear cargo hold.

Although the bulk of the aerodynamic design had been frozen by January 1997, the overall design freeze point still lay a few months off, however, as Airbus continued to press for launch orders. Potential customer SIA wanted more range. In response, the design maximum takeoff weight was raised on both models by 19,800 pounds to 803,960 pounds. Maximum landing and zero weights also grew in response. The increases allowed the −500 to carry 313 passengers an extra

200 nautical miles—or 8,500 nautical miles, with a similar gain for the −600.

In August vital launch commitments were taken from Virgin Atlantic and Air Canada. Virgin signed for up to 16 A340-600s while Air Canada signed for five (two A340-500s and three A340-600s) as part of a wider deal with Airbus covering 21 firm A330/A340s and 20 options. EVA Air of Taiwan later added to the order book, followed by key orders from Swissair, Lufthansa, Emirates, and Air Mauritius.

By December 1997, the Airbus board gave its approval for the full launch of the $2.9 billion A340-500/600 development program based on orders and options for around 100 aircraft, up to 80 of which had been identified. BAe had meanwhile sought $200 million in launch aid from the U.K. government, which had also granted R-R a repayable $300 million loan for development of the Trent 500. BAe was optimistic of getting the money as it was, by then, on course to repay around $600 million (including interest) by 2000 on the original $450 million invested in the A320 in the 1980s.

Launch aid was granted in February 1998. BAe later admitted it could have funded the entire development itself on only slightly worse terms. However, it saw the application as a key test for the government's commitment to U.K. industry in the run-up to relaunch Airbus as a separate company, or single corporate entity (SCE). Under this long-term plan, Airbus was to transform from a consortium into a more conventional company. The new entity was to be called the Airbus Integrated Company and would have two major shareholders. The largest of these with an 80 percent share was European Aerospace, Defence and Space (EADS), formed by the merger of Aerospatiale Matra, DaimlerChrysler, and CASA. The second, with 20 percent, was BAE Systems.

In May, the program received a massive boost when SIA confirmed its selection of the A340-500 with an order for up to 10 aircraft. The order was particularly significant, given the stiff opposition from Boeing's 777X and SIA's prestigious position in the all-important Asian market. The final deciding factor was pricing, as both Airbus and Boeing were able to demonstrate that the aircraft could meet the airline's stringent performance criteria. This critical demand was to operate nonstop all year around on SIA's 8,790 nautical miles route between Los Angeles and Singapore, carrying 200 passengers.

Airbus also managed to stave off desperate attempts by Boeing to overturn the important Emirates order that was finally confirmed, along with the ILFC deal, in September

1998. The two contractors collectively covered up to 26 A340-500/600s worth $3.8 billion, including options.

While the marketing teams capitalized on Boeing's continuing failure to secure launch customer for its 777X, Airbus engineers continued development of the aircraft all over Europe. As the airframe became more closely defined, Airbus also began to put on that most feared of characteristics to any aircraft designer—weight. Rumors of the growing weight problem first emerged at the Paris air show in June 1999. Airbus was tight-lipped about the gossip that told of a study to increase maximum takeoff weight by to 15,000 pounds to maintain performance guarantees. The problems appeared so acute that the range of the models would be around 400 nautical miles short of target—disastrous for some users like SIA.

Around the same time, P&W offered a brief distraction when it revealed studies of a 60,000-pound thrust-geared fan engine internally designated the PW8160. Unlike earlier PW8000 studies, all aimed at the 25,000- to 35,000-pound thrust bracket dominated by the CFM56, the new engine was directed at the growth of the A340 models. Despite almost

The world's longest airliner basks in the French sunshine between displays at the 2001 Paris air show. This first A340-600 was destined to retain its Airbus colors and was used for development and demonstrations after flight tests were completed. The second test airframe, Number 371, was tasked with general development work and engine-related certification. A third, Number 376, was given the job of checking out cabin systems, cold weather operations, and crucial long-haul performance trials.

To increase cargo capacity in the belly, Airbus designed the distinctive new center landing gear to retract forward instead of aft. The result is space for two extra pallets, giving a total underfloor capacity of 14 pallets (10 on –500), up to 42 LD-3 containers (30 on –500), and bulk cargo space. Airbus planned to make the most of this valuable asset in sales campaigns, saying the –600's maximum cargo load of more than 43,300 pounds was 15,600 pounds more than a volume-limited 747-400. Note the nose-down droop of the center leg bogie, compared with the standard trailing wheels-down position of the outboard main gear bogies.

doubling in thrust, the new PW8000 was still based on the advanced core of the PW6000, by then in development for the A318.

Although effectively closed out of the A340-500/600 market for at least the first few years, P&W's alternative engine offered some intriguing incentives. It claimed the engine would give the pair an extra 300 nautical miles range, equaling or exceeding the claimed range of the 777X. This was by now beginning to firm up following Boeing's selection of General Electric's GE90-115B as the exclusive power plant in July 1999.

Later the same month, Airbus confirmed it had asked partner companies to study a 15,400-pound takeoff weight increase, but insisted the move was to provide margin for future growth rather than to compensate for excessive weight problems. Technical director, Alain Garcia, said the rumors

were tied to a "misinterpretation" of the reason for the request, and that the heavier aircraft would be capable of, "around 200 nautical miles" extra range. In essence Airbus was preparing to meet the challenge of the 777X, rather than compensate for weight gain.

Furthermore, Garcia insisted empty weight was "exactly where it should be at this stage. We are within 1 percent of the nominal figure." Garcia's optimism was strengthened by recent wind tunnel results showing, ". . . better than predicted" performance at the low-speed end, and "predicted" figures from high-speed tests.

Airbus was anxious not to repeat the mistakes of the original A340 development effort and worked on a series of aerodynamic refinements to reduce drag to 1 percent below normal. Changes included revisions to the inboard slat, which was given a dog-tooth configuration, enlargement of the num-

Airbus made maximum use of the existing A340-300 design to minimize the cost and complexity of the −500/600 program. For example, sections 12, 13 and 14 of the −600 forward fuselage are the same as for the −300. Section 14 is identical but has the door removed, while section 14B is new and 10 frames longer. The interior was, however, completely restyled with extensive use of light emitting diode (LED) lighting in place of the older halogen bulbs.

bers 2 and 5 flap fairings, and "optimization" of the outboard pylon fairing shape.

However, despite the positive spin put on these developments by Airbus, it became obvious by February 2000 that there was a genuine weight problem. Airbus conceded that both versions of the aircraft were "slightly" over weight, but countered that the wind tunnel tests had been so positive that it expected the A340-500/600 to actually exceed nominal range targets.

The empty weight of the A340-600, Airbus transpired, had climbed to around 3,300 pounds above specification, while the −500 was around 2,200 pounds heavier than planned. The good news, however, was the wind tunnel results that showed range was likely to exceed expectations by up to 1.5 percent at the long-range cruise speed of Mach 0.82. Taking the two factors into account, Airbus figured that the A340-600 would exceed its nominal 7,500 nautical miles range target with full payload by a scant—but vital—20 nautical miles! The benefit for the −500 was naturally much greater with a 60 nautical miles range boost, despite the weight penalty.

The tests also revealed a 2.5 percent improvement in specific range at the higher speed of Mach 0.83, giving the −600 an additional 80-plus nautical miles range and the −500 around 160 nautical miles extra. The overall range for both was less than that achieved at the more fuel-efficient Mach 0.83 cruise speed.

Throughout the 1999/2000 winter in Northern Europe, the parts of the large new aircraft slowly came together. By February, the nose and DASA-built forward fuselage sections for the first −600 had arrived, ready for joining at Aerospatiale Matra's Saint-Nazaire factory. Equipping of the center fuselage section was underway at this site later the same month, while February also saw DASA completing the assembly of the rear fuselage. Meanwhile, CASA of Spain was finishing work on the first horizontal stabilizer box.

Unfortunately, the news from the United Kingdom was not so good. In an eerily reminiscent repeat of the early days of the A340, the delivery of the first seven shipsets of wings from the renamed BAE Systems had shipped behind schedule. The delay was a result of problems met by suppliers to BAE Systems in validating and clearing parts designed using an advanced, three-dimensional design software system called CADDS-5. Some of the suppliers had not been equipped with the software early on in the program, leaving a significant amount of catch-up work to be done.

The A340-600 is so long that special new sensors were fitted to the fuselage to help control bending frequency to within 2–3 Hz. The sensors provide feedback to the fly-by-wire flight control computers, which then signal the rudder and elevator to counter movement of the fuselage. A significant part of the flight control software development and testing was associated with this task and, at the same time, ensuring that it did not compromise the handling capability of the aircraft as a whole.

Rolls-Royce planned a rapid production build-up for the Trent 500 engine to support Airbus' own delivery ramp-up. The projected engine delivery rate consequently jumped from just 20 in 2001 to 150 per year by 2003. Although delayed by the delays in wing production, Airbus hoped to deliver 16 aircraft in 2002, instead of the 21 originally planned. Of these, it believed the last three would be on schedule. The remaining five aircraft, all –500s, were to be handed over in 2003, when the company expected to be back on track..

BAE Systems initiated a recovery program that it hoped would get deliveries back on track by the start of 2001. Some damage to the tight schedule was unavoidable, however. The knock-on effect meant that both aircraft programs would be delayed by three months with a resulting delay to the first-customers. Virgin Atlantic, therefore, expected to receive its first A340-600 in June 2002, instead of March, while the first –500 was expected to arrive at Air Canada in November 2002, instead of September.

The engine story was far better by comparison. The first Trent 500 had run on May 29, 1999, one day ahead of the schedule set almost two years earlier. The engine subsequently performed well in tests and within a few days of firing up for the first time, had been run-up to its full rating of 60,000 pounds thrust. Tests did reveal the need for some changes, such as beefing up of the inner casing around the combustor, which had been deliberately designed in a lighter way to begin with in an attempt to reduce weight.

In March 2000, the first Trent 500 was shipped to Toulouse two weeks ahead of schedule for mounting on the A340-300 Flying Test Bed (FTB). The engine was attached to the left inboard pylon in place of the standard CFM56-5C4 and the unusual combination flew for the first time on June 20. The incident-free, 2.5-hour long flight marked the start of a successful certification effort that ended two and a half weeks early in December 2000.

As part of its "mix and match" philosophy, Airbus used the baseline all-composite fin and rudder from the A330-200 in the A340-500/600. However, because longer aircraft have better natural lateral stability, it was possible to reduce the height of the rudder by just under 2 feet, and the fin area by 16 square feet. The horizontal tailplane, conversely, was extended in area by 38 percent to control the greater pitching moment caused by power variations in the new engines. The new all-composite, all-moving tailplane was made from two carbon fiber-reinforced plastic torsion boxes with a titanium center joint. The pitch trim is the only flight control surface remaining under mechanical control, the A340-500/600 rudder being the first in the family to become all electric.

Although the flight test effort for the engine was due to be completed after 50 hours, the smooth progress of the test bed encouraged both Airbus and R-R to retain it for aircraft-related certification work well into the next year. By March 2001, just weeks prior to the rollout of the first A340-600, the FTB had amassed 150 hours on the engine and engine-related systems, some 80 of which were notched-up in the air.

The tests on the FTB formed a pivotal element of an unprecedented Airbus effort to achieve dispatch reliability levels of at least 99 percent for the new pair after the first year of service. It was, therefore, used to validate everything from a new camera system to aid taxiing and a nose wheel steering damper, to modifications to the flight control system for take-off rotation protection. These changes were needed because of the aircraft's increased size, and tests of the rotation protection system proved so effective that a tail "bumper" was eliminated from the A340-600 altogether.

Although immensely long, the stretched –600 does not appear disproportionate, thanks to its larger Rolls-Royce Trent 500 engines. Seen in flight over Paris, the prototype was to play a vital role in proving two main design targets: speed and range. Thanks to higher engine power and slight aerodynamic revisions, Airbus hoped the big aircraft would have a higher economical cruise speed of around Mach 0.83 or better

Singapore Airlines' order for up to 10 A340-500s was an important boost to the A340 growth program. Not only did Airbus prove it could beat strong competition from Boeing's 777, but the order also strengthened the Airbus foothold in the important Asian market *Airbus*

Work on the flight control system was focused on modifications to deal with the increased flexibility of the larger wing and the longer fuselage. To help the flight control system anticipate the larger aero-elasticity, or bending response of the bigger airframe, the FTB tested a revised system with new pitch-rate sensors on the wings and fuselage.

The maturity program also included tests of more mundane, but equally vital, parts of the design such as the cargo handling system. Here flaws were uncovered that would have caused operators considerable grief had they gone into service unchanged. The cargo handling system was changed from a

six- to an eight-track design with enlarged power delivery units to boost reliability. A full-scale cabin systems integration rig was also built and tested by DaimlerChrysler Aerospace, unearthing more nuisances and avoiding much worse problems later in service.

The cabin was completely restyled and lit by newly developed light emitting diode (LED) lighting, providing greater flexibility in the distribution of illumination. The design was also a cost-saver as the bulbs were expected to last longer than the aircraft! New features also included a touch-screen flight attendant panel that allowed control and monitoring of numerous cabin functions, as well as temperature.

Attention was also focused on the cabin, or at least the exits, for other reasons. Airbus originally designed the A340-600 with six rather than eight full-size Type A passenger doors and hoped to eliminate the two over-wing hatches, required under JAA and FAA rules. These specified a maximum distance of 60 feet between adjacent passenger exits and were introduced originally after flight attendants protested over plans by some airlines to remove over-wing exits on 747s.

Unfortunately, the same U.S. Association of Flight Attendants (AFA) was now threatening to boycott the A340-600 if it was granted an exemption to the 60-foot rule. Airbus believed that it was actually safer not to have the smaller Type III over-wing exit doors because in previous emergencies these had become blocked during evacuations. The distance between the Type A doors 2 and 3 on the A340-600 was 74 feet, which Airbus believed was a better compromise.

Deleting the doors had other advantages that the AFA suspected were the real reasons behind the Airbus move. These included an 1,100-pound weight saving, allowing room for an extra row of money-making seats and reduced manufacturing costs through production-line commonality between the -500 and –600 center fuselage sections.

Although production of the prototype A340-600 went ahead with the initial exit design, it became obvious to Airbus that the regulatory authorities were not prepared to grant the exemption—at least not in the form needed to meet the production deadline. All subsequent aircraft were built with the additional exits. The initial aircraft was not affected by the change, as this was due to be retained by the company as a test bed and would never carry passengers in service.

By September 2000, the first aircraft was practically completed and briefly emerged into the Toulouse sunshine on its way to begin a set of thorough vibration and systems checks. It was not until March 23, 2001, that the prototype was granted its full day of glory, being rolled out in a major ceremony to mark the real start of the next chapter in the A340 story.

Finally, on April 23, Captain Claude Lelaie, vice president of Airbus' Flight Division, and test pilot Ed Strongman were ready to fly the giant aircraft. Pushing the throttles of all four Rolls-Royce Trent 556s to their stops, the crew lifted the aircraft off the ground to begin a planned 14 month flight test program. The 5 hour 22 minute flight was deemed a major success. "We flew throughout the flight envelope from minimum to maximum operating speeds. Despite its impressive size, the A340-600 handled just like any other A330/A340 family aircraft," said Lelaie.

In the euphoria of first flight, it was almost forgotten that those gathered at Toulouse for the event had witnessed the maiden sortie of the longest civil jetliner ever to leave the surface of the planet. In more ways than one it therefore represented a great start for the program and established beyond doubt the coming of age of Airbus.

Passing overhead, an A340-600 displays its new wing that features wedge-shaped inserts to increase its area by 20 percent and fuel capacity by 38 percent. A side benefit of the new wing was that it enabled Airbus to use leading- and trailing-edge components from the original A340 wing with only a few modifications.

Appendix 1: A330 and A340 Specifications

	A330-200	A330-300	A340-200	A340-300	A340-500	A340-600
Length (overall)	193ft 7in	208ft 10in	194ft 10in	208ft 10in	221ft 6in	245ft 11in
Span	197ft 10in	197ft 10in	197ft 10in	197ft 10in	208ft 2in	208ft 2in
Typical seating						
— 3 class	253	295	261	295	313	380
— high density	381	440	404	440	–	474
Max take-off weight (lb)						
— basic	507,000	507,000	606,300	597,500	805,000	805,000
— highest option	513,600	513,600	–	606,300	–	–
Max zero fuel weight (lb)						
— basic	370,000	381,400	381,400	392,400	489,000	529,000
— highest option	374,000	385,810	–	397,000	–	–
Max range (nm)	6,475	4,750	8,000	7,300	8,500	7,500
Fuel capacity (US gal)	36,750	25,765	40,960*	37,380 (39,280)*	56,270	51,680

*with auxiliary center tanks

Appendix 2: A330 and A340 Engine Choices

	A330-200	A330-300	A340-200	A340-300	A340-500	A340-600
Thrust range (lb)	64,000–72,000	64,000–72,000	31,200–34,000	31,200–34,000	53,000	56,000
Engine choices	GE CF6-80E1 (A2/A3) P&W PW4164 and PW4168 R-R Trent 768/772		CFMI CFM56-5C2, 5C3, -5C4		R-R Trent 553 and Trent 556	

Appendix 3: A330 and A340 Orderbook at May 1, 2001

Model/Series	Delivered	On Order	Total
A330-200	85	105	190
A330-300	101	78	179
A330-500	0	10	10
A340-200	28	0	28
A340-300	169	41	210
A340-500	0	23	23
A340-600	0	48	48
Total	**383**	**305**	**688**

Source: Airclaims CASE Database

Appendix 4: A330 and A340 Production List

Serial	Model/Series	Eng.	Delivery Operator	Registration	First Flight	Delivery Date	Notes
001	A340-300	CI	Airbus Industrie	F-WWAI	10/25/91	10/25/91	Flight test aircraft 1991-Current
002	A340-300	CI	Virgin Atlantic Airways	G-VHOL	2/3/92	5/30/97	Flight test aircraft 1992-1997
003	A340-300	CI	Virgin Atlantic Airways	G-VSEA	6/15/92	7/7/97	Flight test aircraft 1992-1997
004	A340-200	CI	Royal Saudi Arabian Air Force	HZ-124	4/1/92	2/28/97	Flight test aircraft 1992-1997
005	A340-300	CI	Air France	F-GLZA	7/31/92	8/17/93	
006	A340-200	CI	Lufthansa	D-AIBF	7/20/92	11/16/93	
007	A340-300	CI	Air France	F-GLZB	1/18/93	2/26/93	
008	A340-200	CI	Lufthansa	D-AIBA	12/7/92	1/29/93	
009	A340-200	CI	Lufthansa	D-AIBB	1/7/93	3/11/93	Sold to Brunei Govt. V8-BKH 1993, to V8-JPI 1996 to V8-AMI 1997. To Jordan Govt. JY-ABH 2000
010	A340-200	CI	Air France	F-GNIA	3/19/93	5/13/93	Destroyed by fire Paris-CDG 20-01-1994
011	A340-200	CI	Lufthansa	D-AIBC	2/3/93	4/5/93	
012	A330-300	RR	Cathay Pacific	VR-HLJ	11/2/92	10/18/96	Flight test aircraft 1992-1996. To B-HLJ 1997
013	A340-300	CI	Virgin Atlantic Airways	G-VBUS	10/25/93	11/26/93	
014	A340-200	CI	Air France	F-GNIB	4/2/93	6/9/93	To SABENA OO-SCW 1996
015	A340-300	CI	Virgin Atlantic Airways	G-VAEL	11/25/93	12/15/93	
016	A340-300	CI	Virgin Atlantic Airways	G-VSKY	12/16/93	1/21/94	
017	A330-300	RR	Cathay Pacific	VR-HLK	12/3/92	1/24/97	To B-HLK 1997
018	A340-200	CI	Lufthansa	D-AIBD	6/18/93	7/10/93	
019	A340-200	CI	Lufthansa	D-AIBE	7/7/93	8/28/93	
020	A340-300	CI	Lufthansa	D-AIGA	9/16/93	12/13/93	
021	A340-200	CI	Lufthansa	D-AIBH	8/6/93	10/22/93	
022	A340-200	CI	Air France	F-GNIC	5/26/93	6/25/93	To SABENA OO-SCX 1996
023	A340-300	CI	THY—Turkish Airlines	TC-JDJ	6/8/93	7/22/93	
024	A340-300	CI	Lufthansa	D-AIGB	10/27/93	11/30/93	
025	A340-300	CI	THY—Turkish Airlines	TC-JDK	6/23/93	8/10/93	
026	A340-200	CI	Government of Qatar	A7-HHK	4/21/93	5/28/93	
027	A340-300	CI	Lufthansa	D-AIGC	10/5/93	12/2/93	
028	A340-300	CI	Lufthansa	D-AIGD	1/4/94	1/28/94	
029	A340-300	CI	Air France	F-GLZC	7/21/93	9/30/93	
030	A330-300	GE	Air Inter	F-GMDA	6/28/93	3/18/94	To SABENA OO-SFM 1997
031	A340-200	CI	Air France	F-GLZD	7/23/93	10/11/93	To Air Tahiti Nui F-OITN 1998
032	A340-300	CI	SriLankan Airlines	4R-ADA	5/23/94	9/19/94	
033	A340-300	CI	SriLankan Airlines	4R-ADB	7/20/94	10/6/94	
034	A340-300	CI	SriLankan Airlines	4R-ADC	3/3/95	3/22/95	
035	A340-300	CI	Lufthansa	D-AIGF	4/13/94	5/16/94	
036	A340-300	CI	Gulf Air	A4O-LA	4/8/94	5/17/94	To SABENA F-OHPZ 1998, To SriLankan 4R-ADD 1999
037	A330-300	GE	Air Inter	F-GMDB	12/4/93	12/30/93	To SABENA OO-SFN 1997
038	A340-200	CI	Air France	F-GLZE	1/24/94	2/21/94	To AOM 1999, Air Liberte 2001
039	A340-300	CI	Gulf Air	A4O-LB	5/25/94	7/18/94	
040	A340-300	CI	Gulf Air	A4O-LC	7/1/94	8/1/94	
042	A330-300	PW	Airbus Industrie	F-WWKH	10/14/93	10/14/93	Intended for Thai Int'l. Destroyed Toulouse 30-06-1994
041	A340-300	CI	TAP—Air Portugal	CS-TOA	11/25/94	12/22/94	
043	A340-200	CI	Air France	F-GLZF	2/17/94	3/18/94	To AOM 1999, Air Liberte 2001
044	A340-300	CI	TAP—Air Portugal	CS-TOB	12/14/94	12/22/94	
045	A330-300	GE	Air Inter	F-GMDC	1/17/94	2/21/94	To SABENA OO-SFO 1997
046	A340-200	CI	Government of Bahrain	A9C-HH	2/25/94	3/31/94	To Brunei Govt. V8-PJB 1994, V8-BKH 1996
047	A340-300	CI	Air France	F-GNID	2/9/94	3/8/94	To SABENA OO-SCY 1997
048	A340-300	CI	Air Mauritius	3B-NAT	4/26/94	5/18/94	To Air Jamaica 6Y-JMC 1999
049	A340-300	CI	Air France	F-GLZG	3/18/94	4/8/94	
050	A330-300	PW	Thai Airways International	HS-TEA	3/28/94	1/20/95	
051	A340-300	CI	Air France	F-GNIE	3/23/94	4/27/94	To SABENA OO-SCZ 1997
052	A340-300	CI	Lufthansa	D-AIGH	6/30/94	8/12/94	
053	A340-300	CI	Lufthansa	D-AIGI	10/17/94	10/31/94	
054	A330-300	GE	Aer Lingus	EI-SHN	2/25/94	4/19/94	

Serial	Model/Series	Eng.	Delivery Operator	Registration	First Flight	Delivery Date	Notes
055	A330-300	GE	Aer Lingus	EI-DUB	3/22/94	4/29/94	
056	A340-300	CI	Lufthansa	D-AIGK	12/7/94	12/23/94	
057	A340-300	CI	THY—Turkish Airlines	TC-JDL	4/21/94	7/28/94	
058	A340-300	CI	Virgin Atlantic Airways	G-VFLY	10/5/94	10/24/94	
059	A330-300	GE	Air Inter	F-GMDD	6/1/94	6/27/94	To Aer Lingus EI-ORD 1997
060	A330-300	PW	Thai Airways International	HS-TEB	8/10/94	12/9/94	
061	A340-200	CI	Government of Egypt	SU-GGG	4/21/94	2/22/95	
062	A330-300	PW	Thai Airways International	HS-TEC	8/12/94	12/14/94	
063	A340-200	CI	Cathay Pacific	VR-HMR	9/14/94	10/26/94	To Philippines F-OHPF 1996, Argentina LV-ZPO 1999
064	A330-300	PW	Thai Airways International	HS-TED	11/25/94	2/3/95	
065	A330-300	PW	Thai Airways International	HS-TEE	1/13/95	1/30/95	
066	A330-300	PW	Thai Airways International	HS-TEF	3/2/95	3/24/95	
067	A330-300	PW	Malaysia Airlines	9M-MKA	2/10/95	3/1/95	
068	A330-300	PW	Malaysia Airlines	9M-MKB	9/8/94	2/23/95	Insurance total loss 15-03-2000 (chemical spillage)
069	A330-300	PW	Malaysia Airlines	9M-MKC	9/28/94	2/10/95	
070	A330-300	GE	Aer Lingus	EI-CRK	10/26/94	11/17/94	
071	A330-300	RR	Cathay Pacific	VR-HLA	8/27/94	3/24/95	To B-HLA 1997
072	A330-300	PW	LTU	D-AERG	1/26/95	2/28/95	
073	A330-300	PW	Malaysia Airlines	9M-MKD	3/8/95	3/24/95	
074	A340-200	CI	Cathay Pacific	VR-HMS	10/27/94	11/28/94	To Philippines F-OHPG 1996, Argentina LV-ZPJ 1999
075	A340-200	CI	Austrian Airlines	OE-LAG	2/2/95	2/28/95	
076	A340-300	CI	Air Mauritius	3B-NAU	10/21/94	10/28/94	
077	A330-300	PW	Malaysia Airlines	9M-MKE	3/21/95	4/2/95	
078	A340-300	CI	Air France	F-GLZH	1/5/95	7/18/95	
079	A340-300	CI	TAP—Air Portugal	CS-TOC	2/17/95	4/24/95	
080	A340-200	CI	Cathay Pacific	VR-HMT	12/5/94	2/6/95	To Philippines F-OHPH 1997, Argentina LV-ZPX 1999
081	A340-200	CI	Austrian Airlines	OE-LAH	2/7/95	2/24/95	
082	A330-300	PW	LTU	D-AERF	11/24/94	12/12/94	
083	A330-300	RR	Cathay Pacific	VR-HLB	2/9/95	2/24/95	To B-HLB 1997
084	A340-300	CI	Air France	F-GLZI	7/12/95	8/7/95	
085	A340-200	CI	Cathay Pacific	VR-HMU	3/3/95	4/4/95	To Philippines F-OHPI 1997, Argentina LV-ZRA 1999
086	A330-300	GE	Aer Lingus	EI-JFK	12/21/94	7/11/95	
087	A330-300	PW	LTU	D-AERH	3/1/95	3/30/95	
088	A340-300	CI	Air Canada	C-FTNQ	1/19/95	6/15/95	
089	A340-300	CI	Kuwait Airways	9K-ANA	3/8/95	3/29/95	
090	A340-300	CI	Kuwait Airways	9K-ANB	3/23/95	4/7/95	
091	A340-300	CI	TAP—Air Portugal	CS-TOD	3/28/95	4/25/95	
092			Not built				
093	A340-300	CI	Air Canada	C-FTNP	3/15/95	6/23/95	
094	A340-300	CI	Air Mauritius	3B-NAV	3/13/95	3/31/95	
095	A330-300	PW	LTU	D-AERJ	4/7/95	5/4/95	To SkyService C-FBUS 1997
096	A330-300	PW	Malaysia Airlines	9M-MKZ	4/12/95	1/11/96	To SABENA OO-SFX 1999
097	A340-300	CI	Gulf Air	A4O-LD	5/17/95	6/30/95	
098	A330-300	RR	Dragonair	VR-HYA	4/5/95	5/22/95	To B-HYA 1997
099	A330-300	RR	Cathay Pacific	VR-HLC	5/23/95	5/31/95	To B-HLC 1997
100	A330-300	PW	Malaysia Airlines	9M-MKF	5/5/95	6/9/95	
101	A340-300	CI	Kuwait Airways	9K-ANC	4/20/95	5/31/95	
102	A330-300	RR	Cathay Pacific	VR-HLD	6/9/95	6/30/95	To B-HLD 1997
103	A340-300	CI	Gulf Air	A4O-LE	6/23/95	10/13/95	
104	A340-300	CI	Kuwait Airways	9K-AND	5/24/95	7/5/95	
105			Not built				
106	A330-300	RR	Dragonair	VR-HYB	6/19/95	7/22/95	To B-HYB 1997
107	A330-300	PW	Malaysia Airlines	9M-MKG	6/22/95	8/9/95	
108			Not built				
109	A330-300	RR	Cathay Pacific	VR-HLE	7/6/95	8/18/95	To B-HLE 1997

Serial	Model/Series	Eng.	Delivery Operator	Registration	First Flight	Delivery Date	Notes
110	A330-300	PW	Malaysia Airlines	9M-MKH	7/18/95	8/29/95	
111	A330-300	RR	Dragonair	VR-HYC	9/5/95	9/28/95	To B-HYC 1997, To Air Transat C-GKTS 1999
112	A330-300	PW	Thai Airways International	HS-TEG	8/29/95	10/12/95	
113	A330-300	RR	Cathay Pacific	VR-HLF	10/3/95	11/24/95	To B-HLF 1997
114	A340-300	CI	Virgin Atlantic Airways	G-VSUN	1/17/96	4/30/96	
115	A340-300	CI	THY—Turkish Airlines	TC-JDM	2/27/96	4/19/96	
116	A330-300	PW	Malaysia Airlines	9M-MKI	10/5/95	11/15/95	
117	A340-300	CI	Singapore Airlines	9V-SJF	8/25/95	10/26/96	
118	A330-300	RR	Cathay Pacific	VR-HLG	11/8/95	12/15/95	To B-HLG 1997
119	A330-300	PW	Malaysia Airlines	9M-MKJ	11/21/95	12/13/95	
120	A330-300	PW	LTU	D-AERK	2/13/96	3/4/96	
121	A330-300	RR	Cathay Pacific	VR-HLH	12/18/95	1/19/96	To B-HLH 1997
122	A330-300	PW	Thai Airways International	HS-TEH	11/17/95	12/20/95	
123	A340-300	CI	Singapore Airlines	9V-SJA	3/25/96	4/17/96	
124			Not built				
125	A340-300	CI	Iberia	EC-154	1/31/96	2/29/96	To EC-GGS 1996
126	A340-300	CI	Singapore Airlines	9V-SJB	3/29/96	4/24/96	
127	A330-300	PW	LTU	D-AERQ	1/26/96	2/27/96	
128	A340-300	CI	Singapore Airlines	9V-SJC	5/30/96	6/21/96	
129	A340-300	CI	China Eastern Airlines	B-2380	3/18/96	5/15/96	
130			Not built				
131	A340-300	CI	China Eastern Airlines	B-2381	5/10/96	5/29/96	
132	A330-300	RR	Cathay Pacific	VR-HYD	3/1/96	4/23/96	To B-HYD 1997
133	A340-300	CI	Gulf Air	A4O-LF	11/7/96	12/4/96	
134	A340-300	CI	Iberia	EC-155	4/16/96	5/10/96	To EC-GHX 1996
135	A340-300	CI	Lufthansa	D-AIGL	4/3/96	5/10/96	
136	A340-300	CI	Cathay Pacific	VR-HXA	5/15/96	6/27/96	
137	A340-300	CI	Cathay Pacific	VR-HXB	6/3/96	6/20/96	
138	A330-300	RR	Garuda Indonesia	PK-GPA	11/21/96	12/18/96	
139	A340-300	CI	Singapore Airlines	9V-SJD	6/10/96	6/27/96	
140	A330-300	RR	Garuda Indonesia	PK-GPC	12/6/96	12/23/96	
141	A340-300	CI	China Eastern Airlines	B-2382	7/5/96	7/25/96	
142	A340-300	CI	Cathay Pacific	VR-HXC	6/20/96	8/27/96	
143	A330-300	PW	Malaysia Airlines	9M-MKY	8/22/96	10/8/96	To LTU D-AERD 1998, To SkyService/Roots C-FRAE 2001
144	A330-300	RR	Garuda Indonesia	PK-GPD	1/9/97	1/24/97	
145	A340-300	CI	Iberia	EC-156	7/31/96	9/6/96	To EC-GJT 1996
146	A340-300	CI	Iberia	EC-157	9/10/96	10/18/96	To EC-GLE 1996
147	A340-300	CI	Cathay Pacific	VR-HXD	7/12/96	9/19/96	
148	A330-300	RR	Garuda Indonesia	PK-GPE	1/31/97	2/25/97	
149	A340-300	CI	Singapore Airlines	9V-SJE	9/4/96	10/17/96	
150	A340-300	CI	Air Canada	C-FYKX	10/24/96	11/19/96	
151	A340-200	CI	Government of Brunei	V8-JBB	9/23/96	10/11/96	To Saudi Arabia HZ-WBT4 2000
152	A340-300	CI	Air Mauritius	3B-NAY	10/28/96	11/13/96	
153	A330-300	RR	Garuda Indonesia	PK-GPF	2/27/97	3/19/97	
154	A340-300	CI	Air Canada	C-FYKZ	11/29/96	12/19/96	
155	A330-300	RR	Cathay Pacific	VR-HLI	10/17/96	11/20/96	To B-HLI 1997
156	A340-200	CI	Egyptair	SU-GBM	11/8/96	11/26/96	
157	A340-300	CI	Cathay Pacific	VR-HXE	11/18/96	12/19/96	
158	A340-300	CI	Lufthansa	D-AIGM	1/6/97	1/28/97	
159	A340-200	CI	Egyptair	SU-GBN	12/4/96	12/20/96	
160	A340-300	CI	Cathay Pacific	VR-HXF	1/24/97	1/30/97	
161	A340-300	CI	China Eastern Airlines	B-2383	1/30/97	3/12/97	
162	A330-300	PW	Korean Air	HL7550	1/29/97	3/3/97	
163	A340-300	CI	Singapore Airlines	9V-SJG	2/6/97	3/1/97	
164	A340-300	CI	Virgin Atlantic Airways	G-VAIR	3/24/97	4/21/97	
165	A330-300	RR	Garuda Indonesia	PK-GPG	3/20/97	4/14/97	
166	A340-300	CI	Singapore Airlines	9V-SJH	3/6/97	3/27/97	
167	A340-300	CI	Air Canada	C-FYLC	3/15/97	3/27/97	
168	A340-300	CI	Air France	F-GNIF	4/2/97	4/17/97	

Serial	Model/Series	Eng.	Delivery Operator	Registration	First Flight	Delivery Date	Notes
169	A340-300	CI	Austrian Airlines	OE-LAK	4/8/97	4/23/97	
170	A340-300	CI	Air Canada	C-FYLD	4/4/97	4/29/97	
171	A330-300	PW	LTU	D-AERS	4/2/97	4/22/97	For SkyService 2001
172	A330-300	PW	Korean Air	HL7551	4/28/97	5/30/97	
173	A340-300	CI	Philippine Airlines	F-OHPJ	5/12/97	5/30/97	
174	A340-300	CI	Air France	F-GNIG	5/6/97	5/28/97	
175	A340-300	CI	Air Canada	C-FYLG	4/30/97	5/28/97	
176	A340-300	CI	Philippine Airlines	F-OHPK	6/5/97	6/24/97	
177	A330-300	RR	Dragonair	B-HYE	6/7/97	6/20/97	
178	A340-200	CI	Egyptair	SU-GBO	6/11/97	6/30/97	
179	A340-300	CI	Air Canada	C-FYLU	4/29/97	5/30/97	
180	A340-300	CI	THY—Turkish Airlines	TC-JDN	8/1/97	8/19/97	
181	A330-300	PW	Austrian Airlines	OE-LAO	8/13/97	1/17/00	
182	A340-300	CI	China Eastern Airlines	B-2384	6/16/97	6/30/97	
183	A330-300	GE	Philippine Airlines	F-OHZM	7/9/97	7/30/97	
184	A330-300	GE	Philippine Airlines	F-OHZN	7/28/97	8/27/97	
185	A340-300	CI	Singapore Airlines	9V-SJI	7/9/97	7/31/97	
186	A340-300	CI	Air France	F-GLZJ	8/22/97	9/16/97	
187	A340-300	CI	Philippine Airlines	F-OHPL	8/28/97	9/24/97	
188	A330-300	GE	Philippine Airlines	F-OHZO	8/29/97	9/24/97	
189	A330-300	GE	Philippine Airlines	F-OHZQ	10/15/97	11/3/97	
190	A340-300	CI	Singapore Airlines	9V-SJJ	9/17/97	10/18/97	
191	A330-300	GE	Philippine Airlines	F-OHZP	9/5/97	9/29/97	
192	A340-300	CI	Air China	B-2385	9/19/97	10/7/97	To Cathay Pacific B-HMX 1999
193	A340-300	CI	Iberia	EC-GPB	10/7/97	10/21/97	
194	A340-300	CI	Air Mauritius	3B-NBD	9/30/97	10/22/97	
195	A330-200	PW	Austrian Airlines	OE-LAN	12/4/97	5/25/99	
196	A340-300	CI	Philippine Airlines	F-OHPM	9/18/97	10/22/97	
197	A340-300	CI	Iberia	EC-GQK	10/22/97	11/10/97	
198	A330-300	GE	Philippine Airlines	F-OHZR	11/26/97	1/26/98	
199	A340-300	CI	Air China	B-2386	10/28/97	11/21/97	To Cathay Pacific B-HMY 1999
200	A330-300	GE	Philippine Airlines	F-OHZS	12/17/97	1/29/98	
201	A340-300	CI	Air China	B-2387	10/31/97	11/26/97	To Cathay Pacific B-HMZ 1999
202	A340-300	CI	Singapore Airlines	9V-SJK	11/18/97	12/11/97	
203	A330-300	GE	Philippine Airlines	F-OHZT	1/16/98	2/10/98	
204	A340-200	CI	Amadeo Corp	V8-AC3	12/12/97	11/27/98	To Brunei Govt. V8-AC3 2000
205	A330-200	GE	Canada 3000 Airlines	C-GGWA	1/20/98	5/29/98	
206	A330-300	PW	Korean Air	HL7552	4/15/98	6/19/98	
207	A340-300	CI	Air France	F-GLZK	12/5/97	1/2/98	
208	A340-300	CI	Cathay Pacific	B-HXG	1/16/98	2/12/98	
209	A330-300	PW	Thai Airways International	HS-TEJ	4/15/98	8/26/98	
210	A340-300	CI	Air France	F-GLZL	1/23/98	2/20/98	
211	A330-200	GE	Canada 3000 Airlines	C-GGWB	3/27/98	4/29/98	
212	A340-300	CI	Singapore Airlines	9V-SJL	2/4/98	3/19/98	
213	A340-300	CI	Lufthansa	D-AIGN	2/20/98	3/12/98	
214	A340-300	CI	Virgin Atlantic Airways	G-VELD	2/25/98	3/16/98	
215	A340-300	CI	Singapore Airlines	9V-SJM	3/13/98	4/23/98	
216	A340-300	CI	Air Canada	C-GBQM	4/28/98	5/14/98	
217	A340-300	CI	Iberia	EC-GUP	4/29/98	5/26/98	
218	A340-300	CI	Cathay Pacific	B-HXH	3/12/98	3/31/98	
219	A330-300	PW	Korean Air	HL7525	5/12/98	6/26/98	
220	A340-300	CI	Cathay Pacific	B-HXI	6/2/98	6/23/98	
221	A340-300	CI	Iberia	EC-GUQ	6/3/98	6/25/98	
222	A330-200	PW	Korean Air	HL7538	7/10/98	8/31/98	
223	A330-200	PW	Austrian Airlines	OE-LAM	7/15/98	8/3/98	
224	A330-300	PW	Thai Airways International	HS-TEK	9/30/98	12/30/98	
225	A340-300	CI	Virgin Atlantic Airways	G-VFAR	5/18/98	6/12/98	
226	A330-200	PW	Korean Air	HL7539	8/21/98	9/8/98	
227	A340-300	CI	Cathay Pacific	B-HXJ	6/9/98	7/28/98	
228	A340-300	CI	Cathay Pacific	B-HXK	7/2/98	8/6/98	

Serial	Model/Series	Eng.	Delivery Operator	Registration	First Flight	Delivery Date	Notes
229	A330-200	PW	Swissair	HB-IQA	8/10/98	9/4/98	
230	A330-200	PW	SABENA	OO-SFP	8/28/98	9/16/98	
231	A330-300	PW	Thai Airways International	HS-TEL	8/21/98	9/23/98	
232	A330-200	PW	TAM Brasil	PT-MVA	10/8/98	11/23/98	
233	A340-300	CI	Lufthansa	D-AIGO	7/17/98	8/7/98	
234	A330-300	RR	Dragonair	B-HYF	10/29/98	10/29/98	
235	A340-300	CI	Olympic Airways	SX-DFA	9/24/98	1/29/99	
236	A340-300	CI	Singapore Airlines	9V-SJN	9/21/98	9/30/98	
237	A340-300	CI	Air France	F-GLZM	9/24/98	10/23/98	
238	A330-200	PW	TAM Brasil	PT-MVB	10/12/98	11/23/98	
239	A340-300	CI	Olympic Airways	SX-DFB	8/31/98	1/29/99	
240	A330-200	PW	Swissair	HB-IQB	10/21/98	11/9/98	
241	A330-300	PW	Korean Air	HL7540	11/12/98	11/30/98	
242	A340-300	CI	China Southwest Airlines	B-2388	11/16/98	12/10/98	For Air China 2001
243	A340-300	CI	China Southwest Airlines	B-2389	10/23/98	11/9/98	For Air China 2001
244	A330-300	RR	Cathay Pacific	B-HLL	11/4/98	11/25/98	
245	A340-300	CI	Air France	F-GLZN	11/4/98	11/30/98	
246	A340-300	CI	Air France	F-GLZO	11/9/98	12/4/98	
247	A330-200	PW	TAM Brasil	PT-MVC	12/7/98	12/22/98	
248	A330-200	RR	Emirates Airlines	A6-EKQ	12/18/98	3/10/99	
249	A330-200	PW	Swissair	HB-IQC	10/23/98	12/11/98	
250	A330-200	RR	Air Transat	C-GGTS	1/13/99	2/23/99	
251	A330-200	RR	Emirates Airlines	A6-EKR	1/26/99	3/31/99	
252	A340-300	CI	Lufthansa	D-AIGP	12/9/98	12/30/98	
253	A330-200	PW	Swissair	HB-IQD	1/7/99	2/5/99	
254	A330-200	RR	Airtours International	G-MLJL	4/6/99	6/15/99	
255	A330-200	PW	Swissair	HB-IQE	1/15/99	2/19/99	
256	A330-300	PW	Korean Air	HL7554	1/5/99	8/30/99	
257	A340-300	CI	Air Canada	C-GDVV	1/28/99	2/11/99	
258	A330-200	PW	Korean Air	HL7552	2/9/99	3/12/99	
259	A330-200	PW	TAM Brasil	PT-MVD	2/3/99	6/28/99	
260	A340-300	CI	Air France	F-GLZP	2/4/99	2/25/99	
261	A330-200	RR	Monarch Airlines	G-SMAN	3/9/99	3/26/99	
262	A330-200	PW	Swissair	HB-IQF	2/9/99	3/12/99	
263	A340-300	CI	Austrian Airlines	OE-LAL	3/5/99	3/24/99	
264	A340-300	CI	China Southwest Airlines	B-2390	2/11/99	3/31/99	For Air China 2001
265	A330-200	RR	Monarch Airlines	G-EOMA	2/23/99	4/26/99	
266	A330-200	RR	Airtours International	G-MDBD	6/4/99	6/24/99	
267	A330-300	PW	Korean Air	HL7553	4/16/99	6/4/99	
268	A340-300	CI	Air Mauritius	3B-NBE	4/2/99	4/16/99	
269	A330-200	GE	Aer Lingus	EI-LAX	4/13/99	4/29/99	
270	A340-300	CI	THY—Turkish Airlines	TC-JIH	3/31/99	4/22/99	
271	A330-200	RR	Air Transat	C-GITS	3/17/99	4/28/99	
272	A330-200	GE	Canada 3000 Airlines	C-GGWC	5/7/99	5/28/99	
273	A340-300	CI	Air Canada	C-GDVW	5/4/99	6/2/99	
274	A340-300	CI	Lufthansa	D-AIGR	4/29/99	5/18/99	
775	A330-200	PW	Swissair	HB-IQG	4/23/99	5/26/99	
276	A330-200	RR	Gulf Air	A4O-KA	5/27/99	6/9/99	
277	A330-300	RR	Air Canada	C-GFAF	6/7/99	1/13/00	
278	A340-300	CI	Air Canada	C-GDVZ	6/8/99	6/28/99	
279	A330-300	RR	Air Canada	C-GFAH	8/30/99	10/15/99	
280	A340-300	CI	Olympic Airways	SX-DFC	7/13/99	10/14/99	
281	A330-200	RR	Gulf Air	A4O-KB	6/3/99	6/24/99	
282	A340-300	CI	Singapore Airlines	9V-SJO	6/18/99	7/8/99	
283	A330-200	RR	Emirates Airlines	A6-EKS	6/23/99	7/7/99	
284	A330-300	RR	Air Canada	C-GFAJ	10/11/99	11/2/99	
285	A330-200	RR	Corsair	F-HCAT	6/16/99	6/30/99	
286	A330-200	RR	Gulf Air	A4O-KC	6/24/99	7/12/99	
287	A330-200	RR	Gulf Air	A4O-KD	6/21/99	7/26/99	For TAM Brasil 2001
288	A330-200	PW	Swissair	HB-IQH	6/30/99	7/20/99	

Serial	Model/Series	Eng.	Delivery Operator	Registration	First Flight	Delivery Date	Notes
289	A340-300	CI	Air France	F-GLZQ	8/3/99	9/7/99	
290	A330-200	PW	SABENA	OO-SFQ	7/9/99	8/9/99	
291	A330-200	PW	Swissair	HB-IQI	7/13/99	8/6/99	
292	A340-300	CI	Olympic Airways	SX-DFD	9/30/99	10/25/99	
293	A330-200	RR	Emirates Airlines	A6-EKT	7/15/99	8/25/99	
294	A330-200	PW	Swissair	HB-IQJ	8/27/99	9/15/99	
295	A330-200	RR	Emirates Airlines	A6-EKU	8/19/99	9/22/99	
296	A330-200	PW	SABENA	OO-SFR	9/17/99	10/6/99	
297	A340-300	CI	Lufthansa	D-AIGS	9/24/99	10/13/99	
298			Not built?				
299	A330-200	PW	Swissair	HB-IQK	9/17/99	10/6/99	
300	A330-200	PW	SABENA	OO-SFS	10/29/99	11/19/99	
301	A330-200	RR	Airtours International	G-MOJO	10/22/99	11/8/99	
302	A340-300	CI	Iberia	EC-HDQ	11/10/99	12/1/99	
303	A330-200	RR	SriLankan Airlines	4R-ALA	10/7/99	10/26/99	
304	A340-300	CI	Lufthansa	D-AIGT	11/17/99	12/20/99	
305	A330-200	PW	Swissair	HB-IQL	10/14/99	11/5/99	
306	A330-200	RR	SriLankan Airlines	4R-ALB	10/7/99	11/15/99	
307	A340-300	CI	Air France	F-GLZR	10/19/99	11/10/99	
308	A330-200	PW	Swissair	HB-IQM	11/9/99	11/29/99	
309	A330-200	RR	Airtours International	G-CSJS	11/25/99	12/10/99	
310	A340-300	CI	Air France	F-GLZS	12/2/99	12/23/99	
311	A330-200	RR	SriLankan Airlines	4R-ALC	11/22/99	12/10/99	
312	A330-200	PW	Swissair	HB-IQN	11/26/99	12/14/99	
313	A330-200	RR	SriLankan Airlines	4R-ALD	12/7/99	1/12/00	
314	A330-200	RR	Emirates Airlines	A6-EKV	12/23/99	1/24/00	
315	A330-300	PW	US Airways	N670UW	3/7/00	3/30/00	
316	A330-200	RR	Emirates Airlines	A6-EKW	1/5/00	1/28/00	
317	A330-200	PW	Austrian Airlines	OE-LAP	12/21/99	2/25/00	
318	A340-300	CI	Iberia	EC-HGU	1/24/00	2/9/00	
319	A340-300	CI	Air France	F-GLZT	2/9/00	2/28/00	
320	A330-200	RR	Corsair	F-HBIL	3/21/00	3/31/00	
321	A340-300	CI	Lufthansa	D-AIGU	2/2/00	2/18/00	
322	A330-200	PW	SABENA	OO-SFT	1/18/00	2/3/00	
323	A330-300	PW	US Airways	N671UW	3/31/00	4/18/00	
324	A330-200	PW	SABENA	OO-SFU	1/27/00	5/26/00	
325	A340-300	CI	Lufthansa	D-AIGV	2/9/00	2/25/00	
326	A330-200	RR	Emirates Airlines	A6-EKX	2/15/00	3/17/00	
327	A340-300	CI	Lufthansa	D-AIGW	2/11/00	3/10/00	
328	A330-200	RR	Emirates Airlines	A6-EKY	3/7/00	3/23/00	
329	A340-300	CI	Iberia	EC-HGV	2/18/00	4/11/00	
330	A330-200	GE	Aer Lingus	EI-EWR	4/5/00	5/9/00	
331	A340-300	CI	THY—Turkish Airlines	TC-JII	3/16/00	4/21/00	
332	A340-300	CI	Iberia	EC-HGX	3/13/00	4/13/00	
333	A330-300	PW	US Airways	N672UW	4/6/00	5/4/00	
334	A330-200	RR	Gulf Air	A4O-KE	4/28/00	5/23/00	For TAM Brasil 2001
335	A340-300	CI	Lufthansa	D-AIGY	5/17/00	6/5/00	
336	A330-200	RR	SriLankan Airlines	4R-ALE	4/12/00	4/28/00	
337	A330-300	PW	US Airways	N673UW	5/3/00	5/18/00	
338	A330-300	PW	Korean Air	HL7584	5/16/00	5/31/00	
339	A330-200	GE	Canada 3000 Airlines	C-GGWD	5/15/00	5/26/00	
340	A330-200	RR	Gulf Air	A4O-KF	4/17/00	5/29/00	
341	A330-200	RR	SriLankan Airlines	4R-ALF	5/3/00	6/15/00	
342	A330-300	PW	US Airways	N674UW	6/19/00	6/27/00	
343	A330-200	PW	Swissair	HB-IQO	5/18/00	6/23/00	
344	A330-200	RR	Air Canada	C-GFUR	6/15/00	6/30/00	
345	A330-200	RR	Emirates Airlines	A6-EKZ	9/13/00	10/27/00	
346	A330-300	PW	Thai Airways International	HS-TEM	6/6/00	7/19/00	
347	A340-300	CI	Lufthansa	D-AIGZ	6/16/00	6/29/00	
348	A330-200	RR	Emirates Airlines	A6-EAA	8/30/00	12/15/00	

Serial	Model/Series	Eng.	Delivery Operator	Registration	First Flight	Delivery Date	Notes
349	A330-300	RR	Airtours International	OY-VKG	6/30/00	7/24/00	
350	A330-300	PW	Korean Air	HL7585	7/7/00	7/26/00	
351	A330-300	PW	Korean Air	HL7586	7/26/00	8/10/00	
352	A340-300	CI	Lufthansa	D-AIFA	6/20/00	8/25/00	
353	A330-200	PW	Novair	SE-RBF	8/30/00	9/29/00	
354	A340-300	CI	Lufthansa	D-AIGX	7/12/00	9/8/00	
355	A340-300	CI	Lufthansa	D-AIFB	8/29/00	10/6/00	
356	A330-300	RR	Airtours International	OY-VKH	7/20/00	8/10/00	
357	A330-300	RR	Airtours International	OY-VKI	8/10/00	9/14/00	
358	A330-200	PW	Air Afrique	TU-TAX	9/8/00	9/29/00	
359	A340-300	CI	LanChile	CC-CQA	9/5/00	9/25/00	
360	A340-600	RR	Airbus Industrie	F-WWTA	4/23/01	4/23/01	Flight test aircraft, first A340-600
361	A330-200	PW	TAM Brasil	PT-MVE	10/5/00	11/10/00	
362	A330-200	PW	Novair	SE-RBG	9/29/00	10/20/00	
363	A340-300	CI	LanChile	CC-CQC	9/21/00	10/27/00	
364	A330-200	PW	Air Afrique	TU-TAY	10/17/00	11/16/00	
365	A330-200	RR	Emirates Airlines	A6-EAB	10/25/00	11/30/00	
366	A330-200	PW	Swissair	HB-IQP			Due May 2001
367	A340-300	CI	AOM French Airlines	F-GTUA	10/27/00	12/1/00	To Air Liberte 2001
368	A330-300	PW	Korean Air	HL7587	11/8/00	11/29/00	
369	A330-200	RR	Edelweiss Air	HB-IQZ	11/8/00	11/17/00	
370	A330-300	PW	US Airways	N675US	11/15/00	12/7/00	
371	A340-600	RR	Virgin Atlantic Airways	G-VGOA			Due 2003
372	A330-200	RR	Emirates Airlines	A6-EAC	11/20/00	12/21/00	
373	A340-300	CI	Air France	F-GNIH	10/30/00	12/4/00	
374	A340-300	CI	AOM French Airlines	F-GTUB		12/20/00	To Air Liberte 2001
375	A330-300	PW	US Airways	N676UW		1/12/01	
376	A340-600	RR	Virgin Atlantic Airways	G-VATL			Due 2003
377	A340-300	CI	Air France	F-GLZU		12/15/00	
378	A340-300	CI	Iberia	EC-HQF		1/16/01	
379	A340-300	CI	Lufthansa	D-AIFC		1/26/01	
380	A330-300	PW	US Airways	N677UW	1/8/01	2/15/01	
381	A340-300	CI	Cathay Pacific	B-HXL		1/22/01	
382	A330-200	RR	Emirates Airlines	A6-EAD	1/12/01	1/26/01	
383	A340-600	RR	Virgin Atlantic Airways	G-VSHY			Due 2002
384	A330-200	RR	Emirates Airlines	A6-EAE		1/31/01	
385	A340-300	CI	SABENA	OO-SQA			Due 2001
386	A330-300	RR	Cathay Pacific	B-HLM	1/18/01	2/15/01	
387	A340-300	CI	Iberia	EC-HQH	1/26/01	3/1/01	
388	A330-300	PW	US Airways	N678US	2/12/01	3/1/01	
389	A330-300	RR	Cathay Pacific	B-HLN	1/25/01	2/23/01	
390	A340-300	CI	Lufthansa	D-AIFD		3/16/01	
391	A340-600	RR	Virgin Atlantic Airways	G-VMEG			Due 2002
392	A330-200	RR	Emirates Airlines	A6-EAF		3/28/01	
393	A330-300	RR	Cathay Pacific	B-HLO		3/30/01	
394							
395	A340-300	CI	SABENA	OO-SQB			Due 2001
396	A330-200	RR	Emirates Airlines	A6-EAG	2/21/01	4/6/01	
397	A330-200	GE	Aer Lingus	EI-DAA		4/17/01	
398	A330-200	RR	bmi british midland	G-WWBM		4/27/01	
399	A340-300	CI	Air France	F-GNII		4/6/01	
400	A330-300	RR	Air Canada	C-GHKR			Due 2001
401	A330-200	RR	SAS	G-WWBB		5/8/01	Leased from bmi british midland
402	A340-300	CI	China Airlines	B-18801		4/26/01	
403	A330-200	PW	LTU	D-ALPB			Due 2001
404	A330-200	RR	bmi british midland	G-WWBD			Due 2001

INDEX